My Visits to the Galactic Council of Heaven

Book 1

Matthew Robert Payne

This book is copyrighted © by Matthew Robert Payne 2017.

No part of this publication may be reproduced, stored in a retrieval system or transmitted in any way by any means, electronic, mechanical, photocopy, recording or otherwise, without the prior permission of the author except as provided by USA copyright law.

The opinions expressed by the author are not necessarily those of Revival Waves of Glory Books & Publishing.

All Scripture is taken from the New King James Version (NKJV). Copyright © 1982 by Thomas Nelson, Inc. Used by permission. All rights reserved.

You can sow into Matthew's ministry, read his blog, view his published books or request your own personal prophecy or life coaching at http://personal-prophecy-today.com

Cover design by Akira007 from Fiverr.com.

Published by Revival Waves of Glory Books & Publishing

PO Box 596| Litchfield, Illinois 62056 USA

www.revivalwavesofgloryministries.com

Revival Waves of Glory Books & Publishing is committed to excellence in the publishing industry.

Book design Copyright © 2016 by Revival Waves of Glory Books & Publishing. All rights reserved.

Published in the United States of America

Paperback: 978-1-68411-252-4

Hardcover: 978-1-68411-253-1

Dedication

The book is dedicated to two of my friends that have walked through this journey with me.

Niels

You have been a wonderful friend to me. We have had many great controversial conversations, and we have learned so much from each other. I have seen you grow from being scared of the future to walking in a lot more peace. You have always been so supportive of me, and through the writing of this book, your support has increased so much more. I love you.

Anna

You found me through my books. We have had some great conversations as well, and you have been so very supportive of me though this project and the one following it. I have dealt with a lot of attacks on my life from the enemy regarding this book, and your encouragement has kept me going. I look forward to seeing you in heaven in the future at one of the seats in the galactic council.

Acknowledgements

First, I want to thank the Holy Spirit, Jesus and the Father for making this all possible. Jesus became the firstborn of the resurrection so that we might be able to communicate with all people that are alive with him in heaven. Without you in my life, my life would have no meaning.

I want to thank all the people who have requested a prophecy from me from my website and all the people who have donated money to my ministry. I also want to thank all of the people who buy my books as these people allow the income to flow into my ministry, which allows me to write, have my books professionally edited and be self-published. Thank you to all who support me financially and who pray for me.

I want to thank my editor, my mother, my publisher, Amazon books and the friends that are in my life that support me.

I want to also thank the galactic council mentioned in this book and all the people of heaven that support me in this endeavor.

Special thanks also goes to Bob Jones, my friend and mentor.

I want to also thank you, dear reader, for taking a chance on me and buying this book. I hope that you will find enough value in this book to continue to follow this series. Be sure to join one of my Facebook groups for updates each month so that you know when each book in the series is free on Kindle for a day.

Contents

Forewords

From Niels

You're about to read an amazing book and about to embark on a journey that will take you into heavenly encounters with a number of saints from the cloud of witnesses. You will need to keep an open mind and allow yourself to be willing to engage with the author in encounters with brothers and sisters who have run their race and who are now in heaven. This amazing book might challenge your beliefs but will encourage you as to what heaven has to tell you. You might be surprised by how saints actually think about us on earth and how intensely they are involved in our lives.

My heart was captured through this wonderful experience as I joined the author on his visits to heaven where he was invited to speak with many saints.

Heaven is as close to us as the air that we breathe, and the cloud of witnesses is watching our whole lives and constantly encouraging us in our Christian walk on earth. I had not realized that it is possible to engage and connect and speak with them in person. However, Matthew's experience shows that this is possible, and as children of the Most High God, we are most welcome to engage with heaven and meet Jesus and the saints in a very personal way.

While reading this book, I found myself increasingly looking forward to each chapter as it filled me with much anticipation and eagerness to read what the saints had to say. I want to encourage you to read this book with childlike faith and an open heart and discover how welcome you are to meet the saints in heaven.

I want to add that you should believe that when you read this book, it has the potential to change you in a positive way. It will create a way for you to engage with heaven and to have your own encounters. It also will be very beneficial to read the book, put it down for a while, meditate on it, pick it up again and reread it. You can do this as many times as necessary so that you familiarize yourself with heaven and the cloud of witnesses. In this way, you create a platform that you can use to ascend and meet Jesus and the saints in heaven yourself. This will help you receive the maximum benefit from it.

Of all the people that I have met and gotten to know in my life and interacted with, Matthew is one of the best examples of what it means to be like Jesus. He is a man very much in tune with his identity in Christ and is literally living it. He has laid down his life and lives for the sole purpose of being like Jesus and introducing him to anyone who desires to meet him. He has nothing in this world but to wholeheartedly live a surrendered life for the Kingdom of Heaven and to tell people that Jesus loves them and that he came to set them free from worldly sorrows and bondages. I believe that this is why he has been chosen to be a mouthpiece of heaven and to bring these messages to anyone who longs to hear them.

I want to thank you, Matthew, for showing us how easy it can be to have encounters in heaven when we humble ourselves and are willing to be open to the Holy Spirit and when we learn how to engage with the cloud of witnesses. My prayer is that this book will bless and touch the hearts of readers and stir up a hunger for more of these life-changing encounters on a personal level and draw them ever closer to Jesus Christ.

From Anna Son-Shine

In the summer of 2016, I was in a season of pursuing God, which meant listening to podcasts and reading books by people that frequently encountered the Lord. The neat thing was God was divinely connecting the dots since these people were all friends on Facebook, and I was becoming a part of their spiritual tribe. I first learned about Matthew Robert Payne in June 2016 when he was mentioned by Praying Medic on his podcast.

Matthew is a prophetic seer that has had conversations with the Trinity, angels and the cloud of witnesses, saints from the past and others that recently passed into eternity. As I read Matthew's books, his accounts reminded me of other people's encounters with heaven, such as Kat Kerr, Lana Vawser and Wendy Alec. As Matthew's books inspired me, I sowed a financial seed into him, and he, in turn, gave me a 10-minute prophecy where Matthew was able to reveal God's heart for me. That prophecy truly changed my life. I then read Matthew's book on prophetic evangelism; before I knew it, I was in Matthew's prophetic group on Facebook, prophesying and edifying other people that are practicing their gift of prophecy.

One day in our group, Matthew started sharing his encounters with a saint that recently went to heaven. As I read of Matthew's encounter, I felt an excitement in my spirit since I immediately knew that he was describing Bob Jones. I faithfully read Matthew's posts, interested in what Bob had to say. It was so reassuring to know that heaven celebrated the things that Matthew did in obedience to God. It was so wonderful to know that heaven cared about the things in Matthew's life, like finding his friend, Blake, at the video store or whether Matthew slept well that night.

Several posts later, I read with bated breath as Bob started to take Matthew to what others describe as the galactic council of heaven. Bob invited Matthew to come to a closed room with 12 chairs in a circle and started naming the people seated in the chairs. Jesus was there with the saints of old. I had mixed emotions when I realized that one of the chairs belonged to a beloved prophet that passed away a year ago, a few days before Valentine's Day. I enjoyed this prophet so much that I subscribed to his ministry website, watched his shows and learned to interpret dreams the Christian way under his ministry. Part of me was joyful because he was living his life fully in heaven, but part of me was tearful because I missed his fatherly presence on his shows. My tears were short lived when Matthew conveyed a message from Jesus, Moses, Bob and this favorite saint to me.

Matthew might be accused of being a medium or of venerating the saints by some readers. I want to reassure you all that Matthew is doing what Jesus has promised us in John 14:12 — we will do even greater works than he did since he was going to the Father. I believe that one of these greater works is to visit his Father's house and meet the Trinity, angels and the cloud of witnesses. Matthew is simply obeying what Jesus told John the Beloved in Revelation 4:1 to "come up here" to the door that is standing open in heaven.

I believe that this door is still standing open in heaven, and this book is an invitation to the reader to come and visit heaven and engage with the galactic council. This book will reveal to the reader how much heaven loves us and is rooting for us, no matter how imperfect we are. You will feel God's heart for his Bride, the Church, and have a glimpse of some places in heaven and conversations with its inhabitants. I hope this book inspires you to live your life with the knowledge of heaven and have a closer walk with the lover of your soul, Jesus.

Introduction

Many people might question the veracity of a man meeting a saint from heaven and dialoguing with him on earth and then being taken to heaven and interacting with saints up there.

First, I want to say that when Jesus himself was here on earth, he spoke to two people that weren't present and alive at the time. On the Mount of Transfiguration, Jesus spoke to Moses, who had died 2,000 years before, and to Elijah, who was taken to heaven hundreds of years before Jesus' life and ministry on earth.

Scripture also records men in white linen talking to the disciples and asking them why they were concerned when Jesus ascended. These men in white linen were not angels, and they told the disciples that Jesus would come back in the same manner as he went.

Also, the Scriptures record that when Jesus was crucified and resurrected, saints from the Bible came out of their tombs and visited the people of Jerusalem.

These three accounts give Biblical precedence to people on earth being visited by departed saints and for it to be possible that this is in the will of God and can be used for his purposes.

For many years, I have had visitations from saints from heaven, and if you read history books, you will find that many Christians that have gone before us have also had visits from the great cloud of witnesses mentioned in Hebrews 12:1.

This book started out with Bob Jones visiting me, and I thought it was going to be a book about his counsel to me. However, six messages into our visits, he told me that God was going to take me to heaven to meet with a council there. From message 7 to message 16 and in the second book to follow this one, I have been visiting heaven to speak to this galactic council.

It is my hope that you will read the whole book and not just skip to message 7. I personally think that if you listen to the counsel that Bob gives me in the first seven messages, you might gain some insight into the type of person that he is now.

As of this writing, I am preparing the second book of this series. I plan to make each book a decent length, so the books will continue for as long as God sees fit to give me encounters.

I prepared this book as best as I could so that I could send it to my editor. Before I sent it to her, I received this prophecy over my life. I think it is fitting to share here as it describes this work and how it is ordained by God. The content was lightly edited for clarity.

Hi Matthew,

As I prayed, I saw a vision of the heavenlies. First, I saw you with the sky and clouds behind you, and within a moment, you transformed into a mighty bald eagle.

The look of this magnificent bird was one of nobility, strength and sheer confidence. Next in my view, to your right, was a pride of mighty young lions running with power and a sense of purpose. They were burnt orange and made of fire.

As they ran, the sky and clouds moved rapidly and simultaneously and the world you were in began to shift into a four dimensional image.

*It was incredible and highly anointed. I hear the word "**access**," and I sense that the Lord has given you access into his Kingdom realm, which is not easily attainable without shedding much of yourself and surrendering to him and his will. He has given you keys into upper realms of the spirit and appreciates your love for him and his holy Word.*

*I feel that he wants you to know that his love for you and your access to him is **limitless.** There is so much more to see and so many secrets he wants to share with you because there's so many more people to reach. Many ministries aren't reaching his children or the unsaved in the unique ways he desires.*

I hope with the two forewords and with this introduction, along with this prophecy, that you have a good idea of what is coming in the pages of this book.

May God bless you.
Matthew Robert Payne
October 2016

Section 1

Visits on Earth with Bob Jones

Message 1

Bob:

It is really good to be with you today. I know that many people will doubt that this conversation is really of God if you are ever called to release this, but for the moment, this conversation is just between you and me.

Matthew:

I am so happy that I have a real spiritual father to come down and mentor me. You were saying as we walked to the shop that you are going to mentor me. I am so happy. I had a man at church that I love pray for a mentor to come into my life, and within a week, here you are! I didn't know that I would be so fortunate to have you as someone to build a relationship with me after the first time you came to see me.

Bob:

Well, if you knew me well when I was on earth, you would know that I would always do the things that the

Father wants. I have fathered and mentored many sons. This is not new to me. I have so much more time on my hands now. I have not been called to mentor too many people on earth. But I am visiting a few people at this time. I am just so amazed at the level of maturity in your life and at the way that you love others. I have been watching you interact with people since I died, and you amaze me.

Matthew:

I didn't know that you were watching me. I knew that you knew about me. But I didn't know that you were watching me.

Bob:

We are called the great cloud of witnesses for a reason. When we are chosen to impact a living person's life on earth, we watch their whole past, their whole future and everything that happens in their life. I bring my experience from many years in ministry as a prophet to you, and I also bring the rhythms and love of heaven.

Matthew:

I am so happy. I was speaking to Elijah the other day and didn't have a lot to say to him because I don't know him well. But you were just recently on earth, and you are so current with this world. I guess without you leaving the earth, you never could have become my mentor now. I am so happy that you are in heaven now and can come down and chat with me.

Bob:

I see you have found the rhythm now, and you are speaking well with me, and you are at peace.

Matthew:

I am just so happy right now. For many years, since 2005, I have wanted a mentor. An apostle told me at that time that I needed one. Jesus told me that he would mentor me at that time. He has done a great job in my life, and I have become very close to him through it all. I have only had Jesus to give me direction. I have had no one else to go to about my decisions.

Bob:

It isn't so cool that I am going to become your spiritual father and that your natural father's name is Bob. And Bob is short for Robert, your middle name. God is so cute how he works like this. Your natural father loves you, but he could never walk you through what we are going to go through.

Matthew:

I am so in love with Jesus. It was though I was bursting last week when I asked my new friend at church to pray for me to find a mentor. My life seemed to be taking off so much that I desperately wanted to connect with someone else. And here I am, typing your name, and then you speak so clearly to me. You speak just like God or Jesus speaks to me. I am so happy that I have such an experienced prophet to teach me and hold my hand and give me emotional and spiritual support. I am so overjoyed. I was so touched when you said about 10 weeks ago that pornography was Satan's last hold on my life and wasn't what defines me. You said I would take off when it was gone. And now, I have been free for five weeks. I am so happy. I am so pleased that you are going to be my friend.

Bob:

Do you remember when you walked through heaven many years ago, and people were bowing to you? You remember you thought that you were having a false vision, so you asked Jesus why people in heaven were bowing to you? Do you remember what Jesus said to you?

Matthew:

Yes, Jesus said that I looked like him.

Bob:

You thought at the time that the answer was related to that verse that says that we will look like Jesus when we enter heaven.

Matthew:

Yes, that is what I thought.

Bob:

I saw you in heaven tonight when you came to look at the Father in that activation by Shawn Bolz that you did. Matthew, you had a friend speak about the glory that is on you some months ago when you go to heaven. She said that in heaven, you shine really brightly. She said some things that you found hard to receive as from God.

Matthew:

Yes, it was hard to receive what she said.

Bob:

You are no ordinary person. You are one of the shining ones of the last days. You are going to plunder and pillage Satan's kingdom on earth. You are going to change the world that you live in. This book might be out in the next six months, and it might take 20 years for your readers to see if this is a true prophecy or not if they can't discern through the Holy Spirit.

But you are going to influence this world in a major way. You remember the prophecy from 25 years ago that said your name would be known like Billy Graham. You have kept that prophecy in the secret place in your heart all these years. You have never stopped believing in that prophecy. It is such a big prophecy, and it has been hard for you to stay in faith and walk it out.

I want to now tell you afresh. Just like Billy Graham was known among the nations, so shall you be.

Matthew:

I know you are a prophet. I know that you know that about me. I have not told you about this prophecy, which means so much to me. Through all the years, I have learned to love.

I have learned to love really well. Do you know I was struggling the other day when people were gossiping? I can't even be around it anymore. Yet the Lord had to do a work in my life even today, telling me that people in the world don't know any better and that I have to excuse them if I am going to sow love into their lives.

You told me at the shop as I bought a Coke that I am such a great lover of strangers. You said that I love so well. That guy at the shop was so excited to see me.

Bob:

You are going to walk in such a measure of glory in years to come that people are really going to be impacted by just meeting you. You won't even have to speak to them. They will be so affected by even your presence.

You are not only going to walk in great glory, but one day, you are going to teach people how to be just like you. You are going to train up whole churches to be lovers of strangers.

In the right time, the right people and the right churches will invite you to teach their people how to be shining ones in their communities.

I know what I have said here has made you think of your book, "Influencing Your World for Christ," also available on a video called "Go into All the World." Heaven wants your "7 Keys to Intimacy with Jesus" book, then the "Optimistic Visions of Revelation" book and then your book, "Conversations with God: Book 2" done.

You have so many books coming out, yet it was so good to watch you listen to 15 hours of Shawn Bolz in 24 hours. I have told you that I want you to listen to everything that he has on his website and in his store. Another book on the prophetic is brewing in you. Shawn will really teach you some great things, and you will pick up something from his ministry.

Matthew:

I love him so much. I don't think he has said anything in the past 15 hours that I disagree with. He is so balanced and healthy. I am just so amazed that the Lord led me to buy his MP3 sets. I have really been enjoying him. I stayed up all night last night listening to him. And

I don't even feel like going to bed tonight. It was so cool. He knows so much.

Bob:

Some people read five of your books and think that you know so much also, Matthew. Some people feel that way about you. They think that they could never know what you know or experience what you experience. So you need to teach them that you are a simple person like them, and if they spend time with Jesus in a meaningful way, they can also have your knowledge and wisdom.

Your job is to demystify it all for them. You are to equip them to do all that you do. You do a great job. This is long enough now. Whenever you want to talk, sit down and open this file, and we will chat in front of your readers. This might not be your most popular book, but many people will like it.

Message 2

Bob:

How are you today?

Matthew:

I have been lying down, but it is not time to go to bed for the night. I then got up and have been wondering what to do. I felt you come and that you wanted to talk.

Bob:

I will be here to talk to you often. I have quite a lot to tell you and share with you. You were thinking about me the other day and wondering what I was going to say. I have heaven at my disposal and the very thoughts of heaven for you. I have so much to share with you. You are a little unknown prophet, but you have a voice. You have people you impact. God spoke to you about how you will reach people that the big names might not reach. If you can handle it, you will also be a big name one day.

Matthew:

Yes, I do look forward to reaching more people. I do look forward to the day where my books reach more people. I know that the message might not change if I become well known. All I can do is speak my heart and share what the Lord tells me to share.

Bob:

You are a wonderful vessel of the Lord. You don't have an agenda to bring your own theology or attract your own following. You have a pure heart, and you are so teachable. God delights in you. You are simple and humble and honestly share when God leads you to speak. Each book of yours is commissioned by God, and you faithfully produce them. You are the pen, and the Lord is your source. You are influenced by the Holy Spirit and angels, and you work each day toward a new book and a new project.

Matthew:

Yes, the Lord leads me. At present, I have three books to produce that need editing, and I am waiting on my editor for the time to edit each of them. I was trying not to have a backlog of books, but I feel that I might have to so that I am not wasting my time waiting. I have more that I need to do. I am so glad that heaven thinks I am a great vessel. I do my best to work on what I feel called to do.

Bob:

You have had a great week talking to your brother. For years, he has been sick and affected by his breakdown, but now, he is back to full strength, and his business partner has everything ready for them to be a success. You can see that the Lord Jesus is behind him and leading him now. You are correct that we want you to advise and direct him from one phone call to the next. You won't have to do much, simply keep him on the right path, according to what you feel is right for him. He is going to impact the world in a great way. The Lord is going to speak into his life, but the enemy will also try and direct him. It's your job to discern what is from us and what is a distraction to him that he shouldn't pursue.

Matthew:

Yes, I have come to realize that this is how I want to be used. I am honored that the Lord sees fit to use me in this way. It's like he is the first person that I will serve as a life coach. I hope that as I grow, more people might come to me to be directed in life through my prophetic gift. I see that Shawn Bolz does prophetic coaching for many people. I guess all good things will happen in the right season.

Bob:

Yes, we are going to use you to give people direction through life coaching. When you have the confidence that you are able to do it, it will happen for you. First of all, we are going to give you the experience that you need with your brother. Jesus is very smart, and he knows how to use you and train you at the same time.

Matthew:

I have to agree. Jesus is very smart and so is the Holy Spirit. I have issues with my confidence, so the Lord is not only going to use me to direct my brother, but he is going to use that to give me experience. I am surprised that God is always taking me higher and stretching me to do more and more. I serve a good God.

Bob:

We have a lot for you to do. You will consult many people in the future. You will bring the love of God and the wisdom of God to them. People who are successful will seek you out for the right direction in business and in life. You have the ear of the Lord, and these people will have a heart to make the right decisions, and they will need you to give them counsel. You have had prophecies that say that you are going to consult famous business people and governments and kings. This is how the prophecy will be fulfilled. You are going to be the person that they come to. You don't need to worry about that now. We will grow your gift and your experience through time. We will raise you up and put you into the right position to start to take on clients. We have everything planned for you.

Matthew:

I am so glad that you have that planned for me. A friend of mine asked if I could do life coaching. I did it for him once. I am happy that heaven knows what I am capable of doing. I have confidence in God and what he has for me.

Note: Since I originally wrote this book, I am now offering life coaching services through my website in addition to prophecies. In the last four months, five people have come to me for life coaching and are happy with the direction they have received.

Bob:

It is not just about you, Matthew. We have people that we want to direct. We have people that want to follow the Lord and who need to check their plans. You are simply going to help them with their lives and the decisions that they make. You will also receive rewards in heaven for the success that they have. I know that I have your attention now when I mention rewards in heaven. You like to store them up. You will simply be the personal coach for people and businesses.

Matthew:

I am aware that this is a place that the Lord is taking me. It is now on my radar, so I will be able to prepare my heart for this direction. I am happy that you are here to talk to me and tell me about this. Thank you for coming today to speak to me.

Bob:

It was my pleasure. I will talk to you again soon.

Message 3

Bob:

How are you today?

Matthew:

I slept in as much as I could. I have finished the three prophecy requests that came in overnight. I always like to hear Jesus speak to people. During one of the prophecies, rather than speaking in the third person, Jesus took over and started to speak directly to a person. It was powerful. I never know what is going to happen.

Bob:

That is the wonder of God. He is in control if we let him be. He knows what to say and how to direct us if we are willing. You are a great vessel and open to the Holy Spirit's leading in your life. You are such a great person with so much to offer. Heaven can do so much through you because you are so open to them. They love you and your childlike faith.

Matthew:

I don't know how I got this childlike faith. It's just me. I am innocent. Even my former girlfriend said I was innocent. I just trust God and let him lead me where he wants to go. One example is speaking to you in this journal/book. I am open to what the Lord wants to say through you, and I am excited to be part of it.

Bob:

We love you. There seems to be nothing that you won't do in obedience for the Kingdom. You live your life out there on the edge of the prophetic. You make us wonder what more you can do. You are so open to the Lord's leading. I marvel at you. Typing and releasing this as a book is radical. But you are radical, and you simply walk hand in hand with the Spirit of God.

It is so good to meet with you each day. I feel that the number one thing a person can do is to be open to the leading of the Holy Spirit. And you are wide open to the Spirit. I ponder how your life will change with my influence.

You have been wondering how your prophetic gift will improve. You want a gift like Shawn Bolz's gift. We want you to relax and rest. We will mature your gift and change it without your personal observation. Don't be so anxious for it to change. We are already using you mightily. We will slowly mature your gift into something more. You just relax and listen to Shawn's teachings and don't fret.

Many people would like the gift that you already have.

I see that you received some feedback on your last post about offering prophetic coaching. People who read that post shared that you would be good at it. See, people that love you know what you are capable of. These people see your potential. We are going to work with you, and soon, you will add another page to your website, offering life coaching.

Matthew:

I can see myself doing that, which will be interesting. I wonder at the sort of sessions that I will end up having with people. It will be very interesting to touch people's lives and direct them according to the Holy Spirit.

I will take your advice to heart about my gift. I will relax with it and simply let God change and improve my prophetic abilities. There is no use in becoming anxious about my gift. Thank you for addressing this in my life. It proves to me that you can hear my thoughts in heaven and listen to what I say on earth. I am so happy that God has allowed you to come and be part of my life.

I am always trying to be and do better. I read to learn things. I speak to Jesus about things. I try my best.

Bob:

You need to learn how to minister and live your life in total rest. You need to learn how not to strive. I am very happy that you live out of rest. It's just that wanting to improve your gift has caused you to strive. We will teach you and lead you. After all, the Holy Spirit is the One that will give you the words of knowledge. You have to depend on him and not on your own flesh. You can't just produce authentic words of knowledge without the Holy Spirit.

We are so proud of you. You are our boy. You are heaven's little champion. You are going to do great things. Many people are going to be blessed through you. We have so much for you. You have so many things that you are going to do.

You are going to travel everywhere in the river of God. You are going to be so deep in the river that when you speak to others, they will feel the Holy Spirit on you. We are going to make you impact everyone that you mix with. You are going to change people. You are going to affect your world and those around you.

We are going to lead you to write about things that are important to heaven. We are going to lead you to read about things that concern us. We are then going to have you write about these things and affect the readers with your books. We are going to make our messages be known. We are going to touch the lives of many people through you.

One day, you might have a best seller that announces to the world who you are. One day, you might have a book that everyone knows about, and then, they will search for other books by you and see that you have written many. I say "might" in this statement as your heart longs for that book, and people have already said some of your books in the past were going to be best sellers, but they failed to produce the desired result. I know that one day, people will know who you are and in that day, many people will start to read all of your books.

You are the voice of God. You are God's mouthpiece. You are under his direction, and you are going to be used to bring his words to the earth. He loves you so much. He has so much for you to say and for you to do. You are so special to God. I look upon his face as he speaks about you. You are treasured by God. He loves how open you are. He loves how you will do anything that he tells you to do. He loves how you delight in him and his Son.

It is so good to be part of your life. When I talk to Jesus about you, I often see his eyes fill with tears. He has so much emotion when it comes to you. He has so much for you to do on this earth. If you could just capture an inkling of what you are going to do in the future, you would cease from much of your worry and anxiety. The future that I have seen for you is far beyond anything that I did on earth. The Lord is looking for hungry ones like you all over the earth. Jesus wants you to speak to the hungry ones and lead them to do great exploits.

Matthew:

You have so much for me. I am humbled by your words. All I want to do is lead people to be the best followers of God that they can be. I long to reach more people. I long to preach. So much is in my heart. I get sad sometimes that I am not being used as much as I want to be used.

Bob:

Everything that has been prophesied over your life will come to pass. God is going to give you opportunities to preach and to teach people about the prophetic. God is going to raise you up in due time. When the time is right, you will receive the invitations, and you will be ready. The Lord is still preparing you.

You have to remember that you are the last wine to be poured out. You are the new wine. Part of the problem is that the world is not ready for you at this moment. The people of God are not ready for the new wine. People are not ready to let go of all their lusts and their love of the world. The world is full of lukewarm Christians, and the church is asleep. There needs to be a hungry cry. There needs to be repentance. There needs to come a desperation in the people of God. There has to be a desire to change.

When the church is ready for the new wine, you will be sent. When the church is ready for reformation, you will be sent. Right now, your message would burst their wineskins. Right now, not many churches could handle what you have to say. You have a unique and pure message. If we sent you now, you would be frustrated that they did not understand or embrace what you have to share with them.

There is nothing wrong with you. I say again, there is nothing wrong with you. It is your message. It is the new wine. The way that we are going to use you is through writing. Through your writing, you will awaken individuals. Over time, people will wake up, and over time, people will invite you who are ready for your message.

You know it is true. Few Christians know the commands of Jesus or are prepared to walk in them. Few Christians know how to live a life that is set apart. Few Christians know how to carry the glory. Few Christians want to let go of their love for the world. At the moment, the church is not ready for your message. The church needs to become desperate for answers.

Just like Jesus arrived in the fullness of time, so it will take the right time for you to appear. You are being saved to bring change when the church wants the change. The church needs to want to change.

It is not that you don't have a relevant message. It is simply that the church is lukewarm and asleep. Pockets of people are awake and on fire, but for the moment, none of these pastors have come across you yet. A time will come when they are ready, and then, they will ask you to come and speak.

I hope you understand this. Many prophets are sad because they have a message and a burden for the people but don't get the opportunity to share. You need to think about the message that you have for the people and write it in your books. Bear in mind that people will be reading all of your books in the future. You need to lay out the thoughts of God and the things that God wants to see happen. You need to think about your books at the moment and not be concerned with when you are going to speak or minister in churches.

Matthew:

Thank you for explaining this to me. I needed to hear it. I see now that it is not me, but the church simply is not ready for me yet. It makes sense. Thank you so much. I will bid you a good day now.

Bob:

See you later, Matthew.

Message 4

Bob:

How are you today?

Matthew:

I slept in today. I am well rested. I am going to church today. It should be fun and enjoyable.

Bob:

We led you to that church. It has many people that are hungry for more of Jesus. It is healthy for you to be in a church that has more people that are seeking Jesus with all their hearts. It has strong pastors and solid leadership within it. I want you to grow and to be in an environment that will help you thrive. The enemy doesn't like you going to that church, which is why he wants you to take so many weeks off.

Matthew:

I didn't know that. It makes sense to me, though. I never took many days off at my last church. I didn't know the enemy was doing it.

Bob:

You are precious to heaven. It is important for you to go to church as often as you can so that you can be filled.

That church has such good worship, and it has a great atmosphere for you. We love to see you being a part of it.

Matthew:

I like the worship there along with the new friends I have made as well. I like going to a place where people love and accept me. I am a little weird, and I have some strange stories. I don't hold back from sharing my stories about my encounters, which makes me hard to get used to. I know that about myself. I just get excited and share everything without filters or masks.

Bob:

Yes, most people wear masks. They seem to moderate what they say to other people for fear of being judged, but you just blurt it all out. You are funny. You don't seem to care if people believe you. You are a strange fish.

Matthew:

I am, aren't I? I am funny. I do not seem to hold back. The Holy Spirit is good at giving me a check about saying certain things, but he doesn't seem to check me that often. I always seem to obey the Holy Spirit when he checks me, but he seems to let me share my wildest stories with people.

Bob:

It is important for you to have the freedom to be who you really are, at least when you are at church. Church should be a place where you can be yourself. A characteristic of the lukewarm church is that people wear masks and put their best foot forward, pretending to be someone they are not. They only share what makes them look good. People that are lukewarm are all about appearances. They like to keep their reputation intact and won't say anything controversial. God doesn't like people holding back. For example, the Bible would not be the authentic Word of God if all the errors and sins that people did were omitted from it. The Bible is right and holy because of all the good, bad and ugly that it contains.

You are less authentic when you can't share everything in your heart with people. You might have more people that you call friend when you hold back from speaking freely, but are they really your friends? Aren't you kidding yourself when you only have them as friends because you are holding back?

Matthew, you remember talking to your friend, Jessica, and she shared that she opened up about her struggles with her friend. But then, her friend didn't want to know her. She told you that when she kept her pain to herself, she had a friend. But when she was honest with her friend and admitted that she was struggling, her friend left her. That is not true friendship. Better to have no friends then phony friends.

The church in general encourages people to wear masks. Because of this, people are not real and authentic with each other. It's a joke. People are not confessing their sins or growing in these churches. People are not advancing but are stuck playing religion. Someone has to stand up and tell the people of God to stop playing and to get serious with God and each other.

You have found people who are interested in being your friend no matter what you say. You could even tell them that you have started to speak to me, and they would not reject you. They might not understand why I am speaking to you. They might think you are deceived, but they would still be your friend. They are solid friends — the kinds of friends you want.

People need to be honest with each other. Part of the reason you can't speak to churches at the moment is that they could not handle hearing about the life that you live. Speaking to angels, meeting and talking with Jesus, and chatting with saints is simply not the "normal" Christian experience. You really are weird. That is why you are so open with us. You have no real friends outside of Sunday at church, so you have space in your life for the supernatural.

Some people say that they want the supernatural, but they have no room in their life for it. God tries to break in with many people, and they shrink back in fear or worry. God would love for each of his people to live supernatural lives and to have saints speaking to them, but the people of God have so many barriers to keep that from happening.

Matthew:

Whatever is happening with others, I am glad that you are here with me. I hope as people read this account with you, they see that you make sense and that it is a good idea to talk to saints. I hope that I can provoke people to a holy jealousy and that they would ask God to have their own mentor come down from heaven.

Speaking of masks, I can't wear one. I guess that makes me unusual. I don't mind people thinking that I am weird. I don't really worry about what people think. I want to find my people — those who are hungry and who believe in the impossible. I want to do life with people that are pressing into the Lord and all he has for us. I don't want to pretend to be something that I am not.

I would hate to live a life worrying about my good appearance. It would be so limiting. I would not have written "Great Cloud of Witnesses Speak" or "Michael Jackson Speaks from Heaven" or even this book if I was worried about what people thought about me. Satan has many people bound up with the fear of man. They are drowning in their own lives because of him and even friends at church don't offer them any relief. In some instances, their friends at church make their lives harder.

I would not want to be like that. I have spent many years without friends, and even now, I don't have a lot of them. I only see people from church on Sundays and don't hear from them during the week. I most often live a life of solitude. That is why I enjoy speaking to you each day. I love having a friend to talk to.

Bob:

It is the Lord's good pleasure to send me to speak to you. I enjoy it. Do you know what I like about you?

Matthew:

What?

Bob:

I love your childlike faith. I see you read about healing, and you say to yourself that when God is ready, he will show you how to do it. I see you read about translocation, and I see you say that when God is ready, he will show you how to do it. You don't dismiss anything of God as too hard for you. You accept that it is possible, and you accept that at the right time, you will be able to do it. I love the faith that you have. It means everything is possible with you.

You don't dismiss things. Even though you need to learn a lot to heal many people, you have not given up on the prophecies that say that you are going to heal.

Even though it seems impossible to translocate from one place to another, you don't dismiss it. You simply wait for the time that you will be able to do it.

I love the innocence that you have. You see a person doing something, and rather than dismiss it and say that is only for them, your spirit embraces it, and you look forward to doing it yourself.

I wish that the Body of Christ had that kind of faith. I wish that the church would see these things and pursue them. I wish that the church would see what is possible and contend with God until they can enter in and do it for themselves. I wish that the church would contend to be friends of God. I wish that the church would draw near to God and get to such a place that the Lord could do anything in their lives.

Matthew:

Yes, that would be great if the church saw something and went for it. It would be a wonderful body if they could all heal and prophesy. The church would then be the answer for the world. Wouldn't it be a great place to live if the world could go somewhere for healing and to receive a message from God?

This church is coming in the future. I can see it even though it seems a long way off. The attitude that you have to be special to heal or to prophesy doesn't help.

The church holds up people as special and gifted rather than training them to walk as disciples.

Bob:

The church needs to learn what is possible. For too long, the church has had "special anointed ones" doing the ministry while the ordinary folks sat on the sidelines.

The church needs to be told that those wrong ideas were given to them by satan. He wants the church to be ineffective and the body of Christ weak and useless. Jesus said that his followers would be able to heal the sick, yet not many believers actually believe that. Even you, Matthew, have only healed a few people. That needs to change. You need to heal people and to teach others how to heal. You need to start to step up.

Matthew:

Thank you for saying that. I might need to reread Praying Medic's book on healing and start to step out in it again. I have been putting it off, but I know that I have been led to read it again. Thank you for your words. I will leave it here now as I need to go to church.

Message 5

Bob:

How are you today?

Matthew:

I am little tired today and have been tired all day. I can't seem to shake it, no matter how long I stay up. Normally, this feeling fades as the day goes by. But today, it is lingering.

Bob:

You were happy when Blake from the DVD store came out to see you today. After he chased you down to speak to you, you saw that he likes you and enjoys your company.

Matthew:

Yes, that was a pleasant surprise for me. It is good to know that he really likes me and will go out of his way to speak to me. I don't know a lot of people, and I look forward to seeing him when I go to the shopping center. I am glad to have a friend there. I am happy that he chased me down, which proved that he really likes me.

Bob:

You have had a pretty lonely life, haven't you?

Matthew:

Yes, I have. I guess that is what makes me so open to having saints from heaven visit me. I know that is why I am so close to Jesus. Loneliness hurts deeply. I was happy my friend, John, from church saw me in my Kebab store yesterday and shared dinner with me. Surprises like that make me very happy. I look forward to days in the future when I might have more friends. I know that no matter what happens, I will be close friends with Jesus. He is good to me. He doesn't leave or forsake me.

Bob:

Yes, Jesus is a great comfort. He is always there, no matter what we do or how correct we are in our theology. He is our comfort and our peace. It is so good to be with him every day in heaven.

It is such an amazing place to be here with him. It's hard to stop crying. His love is overwhelming. So many people that I know up here are so mature and so easy to talk to. On earth, I was kind of mystical and strange and not everyone could understand the place I was coming from.

But here, Jesus has introduced me to people who were very similar to me when I was on earth. I do not have to watch what I say or dumb down how I am speaking for them to understand me. They all understand me, and I feel like Job. When I speak, people treat me with honor and respect. It is hard to explain. But people just get me up here. It's like God has gathered all the people that were truly like me and given them to me as friends up here.

Matthew:

I am so happy for you. That would be wonderful to have friends that understand you. I guess this appeals to me so much as that is what I wish my life were like down here.

Bob:

I have never encountered it as good as it is here. This is surely a place of reward. You are a person who likes the concept of eternal rewards, Matthew. I have many rewards here, but the best thing I have is the quality of the friendships here. I am overwhelmed with the love of Jesus and my new friends.

Matthew:

Do you see Jesus enough?

Bob:

Jesus knows how much we need him, and he meets that need. What is so good about heaven is that you remember every encounter that you have with him. You don't have memories that fade like down on earth. I remember every word and every visit that I have had with Jesus since I have been here. He adds something to you every time you meet him. You truly do go from one glory to the next when you are here.

Matthew:

This makes me cry, Bob. I am so emotional now. I can see it, and I wish that it were my life. I so long to go to heaven. I have a hard time visiting heaven in visons as it is so hard to come back to earth. You speak, and I see it.

Bob:

You have an important job to do on earth now. You have so many rewards in heaven. The people in heaven love you. I have met your sisters and seen the gallery that your sister has with all the paintings of you. I have learned a lot about you here. Your sisters love you so much. Like I said, the people of heaven love you so much. You are going to have such a wonderful time here. You will make great changes on earth. You are a gift to the world. You know the name "Matthew" means "gift of God." You really are becoming a gift to the world.

You worry a little about what books you will write in the future. The enemy has been harassing you on a number of fronts. He is not going to win. You are going to overcome, and you will go on and make a difference with what you write. You need not cry, my son. It's all going to be okay.

You need to get through your struggles and overcome so that you can be an example to others. I have a lot of time for you, dear son. You have such a big heart, and you are such a great vessel. Heaven has many things to say to people on earth. You can write many books with saints speaking to people on earth.

You are going to make it.

Matthew:

I have to go out now. Thank you for your comforting words.

Bob:

Have a good night. Remember, heaven goes with you. How did you like the babies staring at you today? They can see the glory on you.

Matthew:

It's always good to see the children staring at me. I know that they see the glory. They think I am an angel. That touched me today also. I am sorry that I was so sad earlier.

Bob:

It's understandable, Matthew. God knows what he is doing through these encounters. I am going to go out with you tonight. Love you.

Message 6

Bob:

How are you today?

Matthew:

I have slept well and long. The dreams weren't fun, but I have recovered from that. I gave a strong prophecy to someone today. The person will move in revival, and he is full of the light of Jesus. It was a real honor to speak to him and prophesy over him.

Bob:

It is so exciting to find out about a person while you prophesy, isn't it? God shows you their heart, and your own heart goes out to them. You can see part of them and be warmed spiritually by what you see. The world is made up of many Christians with great potential and who are full of the light of Jesus. I know how you felt as you prophesied. I felt it also.

Matthew:

It is so refreshing to meet people who shine with the love of God. I so enjoy meeting them, even if only through a prophecy that they have requested. I am happy to meet people who love God with all their heart and who demonstrate the love of Jesus to the world around them. I noticed you said that you felt how I felt when I prophesied. It amazes me that the Lord lets you feel my feelings. I love and serve an amazing God.

Bob:

That amazing God thinks that you are someone special. The Lord God loves you so much. He told me to come and see you today and tell you that he is very proud of you. He wants you to know how special you are to him. He does not think you are ordinary; he knows you are extraordinary. You are one special man of God who has big dreams and walks and talks with the saints. God wants you to learn to walk like Enoch. God wants you to visit him in heaven more often then you currently do. God misses you. He wants you to walk in the heavenlies and be blessed by the company of heaven.

God wants your life to go from normal to totally supernatural. He wants to take you away. He wants you to live with him and walk with him and his saints in heaven. He cares for you and wants to teach you directly. He wants to counsel you so that you can meet some of the most important people in heaven.

Matthew:

This is all news to me. I know that Enoch had an amazing supernatural life. Just to have God mention his name in connection with my name means a lot to me. I love God and want to please him. I want to make him happy. Can he arrange for the saints to come here instead of me going to heaven?

Bob:

You know that he could arrange that. But I feel that he wants you to walk in the atmosphere of heaven. I believe he wants you to relax and travel to heaven and make a conscious effort to go there. He wants to teach you, and he wants you to meet his champions up there so that they can speak into your life.

You have a different life ahead of you. You are not created to be ordinary. God wants to impart his wisdom into you. He wants you to be like Moses and lead the church out of slavery and into the Promised Land. God wants to use you like John the Baptist to prepare the church to meet their groom. What you need to do is counter-cultural to the way the church is acting and behaving now. We need you to sit in councils in heaven and learn the will of God for the church for the future, and then, we need you to bring the voice of heaven to earth.

This is more important than your personal comfort and more important than your worry about going to heaven and not wanting to come back to earth. We need you to virtually live in heaven over the coming years. You are going to be taught in that atmosphere and then bring back the messages to earth and release them in prophetic words and in the books that you write.

I will be with you every time that you go to heaven. I will be there speaking and observing what you are learning.

You are going to learn to be an extraordinary prophet. You are going to be other worldly and a citizen of heaven as well as of earth.

Matthew:

I don't know if I would have thought of this without you telling me here face to face. It is a little deep to be compared to Moses and John the Baptist. I fully understand your meaning. The church, by and large, is in Egypt and in slavery with the world system. Very few Christians have the faith to live in a world without money. I know a lot of work needs to be done. I guess that I will need to learn so much in heaven.

I think that if I spend time there, it will increase my burden for the church and the people of God. I have to trust that my heart will be able to cope with it. I think I will have to type out what is said in heaven so I can read it and reread it so that I can understand it. I am not even sure if I would publish it. I guess people would glean from it. Now I know why I had to read Praying Medic's last book. That was preparation. It is just overwhelming to me.

This is all amazing revelation. In general, people do not realize what has to happen before Jesus comes back. I think that we have a situation of the blind leading the blind. I cannot understand why the church is asleep, but they think that they are awake. I guess this is the reason why I need to go to heaven. I can see myself sitting at my keyboard and typing and having visions and conversing with the saints. I can see the wisdom in getting away from the earth so that I can gain a proper perspective.

I think of my own church. They are good people with great leadership, but I guess that they would not consider that they are lukewarm or blind or that they are asleep. It is hard to see these things for yourself, but I sense them in my core, my inner self, and I see them plain as day. It makes me so sad. So few people seem to be really awake in the Kingdom.

I am sad, Bob.

Bob:

You are just sensing the corporate feelings of heaven. The church of God has so much potential, and this potential is found in the very teachings of Jesus, but they are so far from what he taught. The church, even the grace-preaching church, is so far from the ideal and what Jesus wants for his Bride. The world needs to come to know Jesus and not just religion. The world doesn't need to see a people of God that are bound up with religion.

I will let you go as I see that you have been overcome with sadness.

Matthew:

See you later, Bob. This sadness is overpowering.

Section 2

My Visits to the Galactic Council with Bob

Message 7

Bob:

How are you doing tonight?

Matthew:

I was trying to go back to sleep when you came into my room and told me to get up and do this latest post. I have no idea of what you are going to say, but I am excited to speak to you today. I heard Shawn Bolz speaking about you today, and he seemed to know you very well. He said you used to speak for hours. He said you had the gift of the gab. Has that changed in heaven?

Bob:

What many people don't know about heaven is that you keep your personality and your soul when you go there. Sure, you become a better version of yourself, but you stay the same in many respects. I still love to talk. I learn so much as I speak. I used to speak a lot, and I still do. I have a lot of wisdom and now, in the atmosphere of heaven, things have only become more exciting.

I have so much more to talk about now. It's amazing when you don't have to sleep. It is exciting to go to a lecture by Isaiah and hear him speak about the prophecies of the future of the earth and how they are now coming into play. Then, I can attend a private heavenly council meeting and speak in more detail about these same prophecies.

It is fascinating to have your heart desire for something on earth to change and then, to be able to listen to all the prayers that are coming from earth for that same desire. It is amazing to be in a place with so much information.

I love my life here. I am so glad that I can come to earth and deposit something into the people of earth who are open to meeting me and hearing from me. My life is so exciting.

Matthew:

You make my heart sick. I wish I were there with you. I wish I could experience it like you are experiencing it.

Bob:

You can, Matthew. You can come here anytime by training yourself. If you are open and disciplined, you can visit here and interact with us. Even as I was speaking right now, you were in heaven watching me.

When I spoke about lectures of Isaiah, you came into the room and watched me. When I spoke about listening to the prayers on earth, you saw me doing it. It just comes down to your imagination and your concentration.

You see this water? Do you see the people swimming? Do you see the sand? Do you feel it between your toes? Do you see how people are looking at you? Do you see how they know that you are from earth? Do you see them listening to what I am saying?

Now come here. Do you see that we are now in a closed room with 12 chairs in a circle? Do you see Jesus? Do you hear the names? Moses, Paul, John the Baptist, John the Disciple, Elijah, Enoch, John Paul Jackson, Isaiah, Malachi, Peter and I make up the 12 seats.

You are here. You are in a heavenly council room.

Jesus:

Welcome, Matthew. It is good to have you here. We are excited to meet you. We have been waiting for you.

Matthew:

I am almost overcome with tears. It is so good to meet such important people. I am overcome to meet Isaiah. I love his book.

Isaiah:

You love the book I wrote. I wrote that book for you. I love you. You are a champion and such an overcomer.

I love you. There is so much glory on you. You are the future. I wrote about people like you. I have much to tell you. I have so much information to share with you as you read my book again. I love you so much. You need not fear that you won't understand what is happening in the book. I know what it means. I will show you what is relevant to you and the people of the earth now.

Matthew:

I love you, Isaiah. My eyes are filling with tears. You wrote the most excellent book. It is my favorite book in the Bible. It has so much about who I am in there. It has my purpose outlined there in these verses in Isaiah 42:6-9:

"I, the Lord, have called You in righteousness, and will hold Your hand; I will keep You and give You as a covenant to the people, as a light to the Gentiles, to open blind eyes, to bring out prisoners from the prison, those who sit in darkness from the prison house. I am the Lord, that is My name; and My glory I will not give to another, nor My praise to carved images. Behold, the former things have come to pass, and new things I declare; before they spring forth I tell you of them."

This sums up my life purpose, and it was also the purpose of Jesus. You are showing me new things right now. I am so excited to speak to you.

Isaiah:

I am excited to speak to you as well. You are a treasure in an earthen vessel. You make the Bible look good. Jesus had you in mind when he spoke of being his light on earth. You are a great light. You are going to say many things. You are going to write many great books. Many people are going to come to your light. I have so much to say to you and many things to show you in the Word of God. I am so overcome with joy to meet you and speak into your life.

Bob:

Now, how is that, Matthew? You have a room full of people to talk to. These people will make up your council and together, you will speak about matters and take actions that will affect the future of the earth. You have been tried and tested by fire. You have overcome, and now, you are a vessel that we can use.

Matthew:

It is true that the Kingdom is a place where we walk by faith and not by sight. I could have never imagined coming to a place with these people in it. I never thought I would be worthy to meet and interact with people like this for a valid purpose. If you had not told me last week that this was going to happen, and if two people had not prophesied that this was going to happen, I am not sure that I could be doing it. It seems that everything is planned in advance for me.

Bob:

I don't want to overwhelm you. You can speak to and interact with all of these people, and everything that you ask and say was planned by God before the foundation of time.

Jesus:

I have many great things for you to see and do. We are going to talk to you and share things with you. You can come here anytime and be blessed and do what we want you to do. We have all the time in the world, and every interaction that you have will be done the same way. You will be on earth listening to us and typing what we say, and readers will read what you type. If you are typing, you can see and reread it, and people can be taught by it besides what we do with you and through you.

Matthew:

Elijah, I am overcome to meet you. I know that we have met a few times before, and I even interviewed you in my book, "Great Cloud of Witnesses Speak," but to think that I can come to this room and speak to you each time I sit down to speak with Bob is overwhelming. I am producing my book, "Optimistic Visions of Revelation," now, which speaks about your future role on earth, and

I am just overcome that I have the honor of speaking to you.

Elijah:

Do not marvel at the opportunity to meet and interact with me. This is part of your purpose on earth and what God planned for your life. You have just the right combination of childlike faith and innocence to believe that this can happen and to do it. God is a wonderful God. He has chosen you. Whether you know it or not, your heart is an amazing heart, full of love, and as a prophet, you can be used to bring heaven's decrees and words to earth. If you had never agreed and if you had not gone through the process of producing "Great Cloud of Witnesses Speak," this would not have happened this way. Heaven set that test for you. Two other men were given that task and turned it down due to fear of man.

Now we have you. Now it is time for you to come here often. It will take some time for you to speak to all of us and grow in your relationship with all of us before we get down to the business that is at hand. Yet, as you speak to us and as we speak to you, the messages will be interesting to read.

One thing that you have noticed and thought about right now is the fact that we all speak your language and speak with words that you are used to. Some people might doubt that we are speaking because of this, but those people are not our concern. We know the people we want to reach, and no matter who reads this, the most important thing is for you to type our words so that you can read and reread them and grow in relationship so much that when it comes time to make decisions and take the necessary steps, you will have the faith and courage and the will to do it.

Matthew:

That makes sense. I can see this will be quite a number of books. It will take many conversations to get to know everyone. It will take much research for me to look into the saints more to understand them more. I can see that this is a major work. I can see that the title of the book might be, "My Visits to the Galactic Council of Heaven."

Bob:

Just as Jesus is the door to heaven, I have become a gate that you are going to access to come to this room. As we visit, you will grow in many ways, and we will get to know each other more. I will speak to you from time to time throughout your days, and each time that you are going to come here, I will bring you. Have a good night, Matthew. See everyone in the room waving and hear them all saying goodbye.

Matthew:

Bye, Bob. Thanks for this experience.

Message 8

Bob:

How are you today?

Matthew:

It's the middle of the night. I couldn't stay asleep, so I got up. My website designer updated my new page that offers life coaching to people. You will remember that you told me to do that in one of your former messages. I have finally gotten around to it after people prophesied about new windows of heaven opening to me.

Bob:

I will tell you to do many things that you will do. I am glad that you have done that. This will give God a further way to be able to bless you. Are you ready to ascend?

Matthew:

Yes, I am.

Bob:

You are now at the Crystal Sea. Here is Niel's mother. Your friend, Niels, asked you to say hello to her if you see her. She has something to say:

"Tell Niels that I love him more than I ever loved him. I am enjoying myself up here, and I have many friends. I enjoy learning all that this place has to teach me. I have a great big garden at my house that keeps me busy. Heaven doesn't have weeds, so I don't have to do weeding. I speak to many people here. Everyone is so loving and friendly.

"Friends are different here. People know you for who you are without judging you or wearing masks. I am overwhelmed at what close relationships I have with my new friends.

"There is a oneness here. Everyone is one. It is hard to explain in earth language. But everyone loves each other, and we are connected mystically to Jesus. We are all one together.

"I am learning so much and with everything I learn, my heart grows closer to Jesus. It is the best feeling in the world, the ability to be one with Jesus. I wish that you could understand, Niels, that Jesus really adores you, and you will be safe to come here without worry.

"It was great to talk to you, my love. Please know that I have seen your whole future, and one day, you will know so much and yet be at peace with who you are. One day, you are going to teach others who fear how to walk in freedom. I will continue to pray for you. If you ever want to contact me, just tell Jesus what you want me to know.

"I miss you. Bless you."

Matthew:

That makes me cry, Bob. I don't know Niel's mother's name, but I know he will be happy to hear from her. He asked me to say hello to his mother if I ever met her. I had no idea that this was going to happen. I am so happy for Niels.

Bob:

We have one more visit for you. Here we are at the park, which you know is full of children that were aborted on earth. Here is Rebecca, who you spoke to 10 years ago.

Rebecca:

Hi, Matthew. It is so good to see you today. You can see I am a young woman now. I am pleased to report that your son is now hungry for the things of God. I have been watching him. He is not the most full-on Christian, but he is understated. He is serious about his faith but without pretense. He is growing with the Lord, and he is very much in love with his wife. He has a heart to serve God, yet he does not want to be fake in any way. This desire not to be fake holds him back a little, but we have wonderful plans for him up here.

He has prayed some big prayers, and heaven is excited for him. You might never be close to your son, but we will keep you updated. It makes me so glad that you have been invited to the council. I have been praying for you all this time. I have been interceding for you as well as for your son, Brandyn.

I love your innocence. I see you looking at my beauty, and I see it stir a desire in your heart for a wife. I love you, Matthew. God has that planned for your life. I love praying for you. I pray that you can stay strong while you wait for her.

I am exquisite, aren't I? I see that you are amazed at my beauty. I am your friend for life. I love you so much. You and your son are part of my project. You are like a father to me. I am glad that you are impressed with me. God has been really good to me to allow me to grow up to be so pretty. I long to meet you more. Please stop in and see me as Bob leads you.

Bye for now. Remember I am praying for you every day. You don't have to worry so much about intercessors on earth. All of the people in heaven pray for you. If you look, the thousands of children that are here know of you and are waving at you. One day, I will introduce you to some of them that would love to talk with you.

Matthew:

Give me a hug, Rebecca.

(We hug.)

Rebecca:

Don't forget this hug, Matthew. This is what real love feels like. This is life giving. Your wife will love you like this. Love you heaps. Bye for now.

Bob:

Come on, I have somewhere else to take you.

Can you see the throne and hear God calling you up to his Son's throne?

Matthew:

Yes.

Bob:

Go on, walk up the stairs and meet him.

Matthew:

(I walk up the stairs to the throne of Jesus and sit down, overwhelmed by the glory in the room.)

Father:

Hi, Matthew.

Did you enjoy meeting Niel's mother and Rebecca?

Matthew:

Yes. It was comforting to meet them both. I thought I was going to come straight to the council room, but it looks like you had different plans. I didn't know Rebecca was still looking over my son's life and praying for him.

I am so glad that she told me how he is doing. He doesn't really respond to my emails.

Father:

Do you remember our last conversation when you sat on my Son's throne?

Matthew:

Yes, it is burned into my memory. You told me to let you control my life.

Father:

And how do you think that is going?

Matthew:

Your Holy Spirit directs me very well as does Jesus. I think I am doing the best that I can.

Father:

Yes, you are doing a great job. Today, I am giving you an upgrade in your anointing. You make me so happy and proud. You are so submitted to us. I am so pleased with everything that you do. I could not be happier with you. Did you hear that? I could not be happier with you.

You are in a sweet spot with us. You are an individual. Don't try and be Shawn Bolz who you admire so much. It's good to pursue his gift, but we are the ones that will give you that upgrade. I am so happy with who you are. I could not be happier with you. That is three times now I have told you that. When the naysayers come in and mock you, when your critics come, you can remember that you met me and that I said that I could not be happier with you.

You are living 1 John 2:6 now. Put it into the text here so that people can read it. I will wait for you to do that.

"He who says he abides in Him ought himself also to walk just as He walked."

This is not a future verse for you to move into and develop in your life, Matthew. I watch everything that you do, and you walk like my son, Jesus. I am so proud of you. I want you to know that you are my messenger. You are my prophet. You are my mouthpiece. You are my hands and feet on earth. I want you to know that you are cherished by me. I want you to know that you are Israel to me. Those that bless you will be blessed. Those that act against you will be brought low. People that do anything to bring down your name and your reputation will be dealt with by me and my angels.

You do not need to worry about your life. You can walk in love toward those that speak against you. You can keep your peace. And you need not pray for people to be blessed that send you money. I will personally bless those that bless you. I will personally reward anyone that shows you favor. I will bless them financially; I will open doors for them; I will give them breakthroughs. Just like people who bless Israel are blessed, so, too, people who bless you will be blessed.

I want you to know that you are on the right path. I want you to know that you are doing everything that I want you to do. I want you to know that you are in my perfect will. I want you to know that I will always lead you in the way that you should go and if you miss my leading, I will have another person prophesy the direction to you.

I want you to teach my people that they, too, can know me and walk in my favor. I want you to lead people to me. I want you to encourage others to know me. You have seen how June has taken off toward me. I want you to be an encourager and a catalyst for people to seek me.

You are wonderful. Now, give me a hug.

(I hug Father, and he holds me close.)

God:

Go get them for me, Matthew!

Matthew:

I will, Father.

Bob:

That is your visit today, Matthew. You never got to see the council. I know that you are happy and blessed. I love you, my brother. I am so excited about my assignment in your life. I heard what God said to you. Just remember that God could not be happier with you. Okay, now back to earth you go.

Time for you to make another coffee. Love you. Bye.

Matthew:

Bye, Bob.

Message 9

Bob:

Hello, Matthew. Once again, it is the middle of the night, and you are up. I can see you are looking forward to ascending to heaven. You have some good music on, you are at peace, and I am here. How are you feeling?

Matthew:

I am excited and scared at the same time. I am in a "funny" mood. It is funny to have people reading these encounters. It makes me a little more accountable. I'll get used to it, but I thought I would mention it.

Bob:

It's just like your jacket, Matthew. When you put it on, it feels a bit tight, but after a few hours, you don't notice the tightness. It is going to be same as you ascend and speak to the council. Before you go, you might be nervous, but in the midst of the interaction, you will always be comfortable. Ready to go?

Matthew:

Yes.

Bob:

Well, here you are at the door. Jesus has prepared a table and welcomes you. Fruit and drinks are set on the table, and the 12 have taken their seats. Have a seat next to me.

Matthew:

Thank you, Jesus, for inviting me.

Jesus:

This is your heritage. This was written down on the scroll of your destiny. We are merely doing what was planned for you. Of course, you didn't know it was going to happen to you, but many times, we have surprises for people.

The people in this room have much to say to you and to discuss with you. They all know that their words are going to be typed up and made into books. So some of what you hear might not just be for you but might be going to have a bigger impact on one of the future readers of the book that you produce.

Matthew:

I can understand that. When I produced, "Great Cloud of Witnesses Speak," I had no idea that it was going to affect people like it did. One lady wrote to me and said Leah's interview made her weep. I know you have divine purposes for what is said. Just like the apostles wrote to the churches in their day, and today, everyone is still being blessed by what they wrote to people back then.

I guess I will mention the people in the room for the readers. We have Paul, Peter, Elijah, Enoch, John the Baptist, John, Malachi, Jesus at the head of the table, Isaiah, Moses, and the two contemporaries, John Paul Jackson, and Bob, as well as me. We have 13 altogether.

Paul:

How do you feel, Matthew? Do you feel worthy to be here with us?

Matthew:

I am very close to Jesus, Paul. I strive to be as close to him as possible. Of course, I feel humbled to be here. But, yes, I feel worthy. I am emotional now that you asked me. Who of us is really worthy?

Paul:

There is none worthy without the shed blood of Jesus. And because of that blood, we are all made worthy. None of us were righteous enough to come to heaven. It's a good feeling to be loved and brought close. I don't understand why Jesus chose me. It took me years to come to grips with it.

It leaves us all thankful for the grace and love of God.

Matthew:

It is so good to see the memory of your life. I hold you in such high esteem. I don't know how you coped with your beatings and sufferings. You didn't stop but kept on going. I don't know if I would have continued if it had been me.

Paul:

And yet here you are in the same room with me. That must say something to you. You have suffered your share. Through your loneliness and your suffering, you drew close to Jesus. You should hear how Jesus speaks about you to us.

Matthew:

(I look to Jesus, who has a tear running down his cheek. I have seen Jesus shed a tear before because of my friend's unbelief, but I never thought I would see him cry about me.)

Jesus, are you crying because of me?

(Another tear trickles from his eye and travels down his face. He nods.)

John the Baptist:

Jesus is crying because of you and because of his love for you. But it is more than that, Matthew. He is thinking of his Bride that he loves. He is thinking of his children also coming to see him in visions. He longs to meet his Bride. He longs for you to be a forerunner of people that come to heaven.

Matthew:

Thank you, John. I see you can read Jesus' mind here. I guess that is why you are part of this council. I have a calling to bring the Bride home and prepare them to meet Jesus, their Groom. I have a calling like yours.

John the Baptist:

Yes, I am in the room for more than one reason. But that is a large part of why I am here. I have some things I want to say to the people of earth through your books. I didn't have much recorded in the Bible, and I have so much more to say to this generation.

It is so good to meet you. You are worthy to be in this room. We are really here. We are not in two places at once. We are actually here to speak to you. You have been selected to be a mouthpiece for us.

I want you, the reader, to understand that heaven is open to you. I want you to know that there is nothing but faith stopping you from coming to heaven. I am seated halfway down the table directly opposite Matthew. Between us is a pitcher of wine and a big bowl of grapes. I have a short, trimmed beard, and I am in royal purple with a white turban on my head.

Can you imagine me as I speak to you? If you can see and hear me, you are here with us. Come along and keep reading and use your imagination, and soon enough, you won't just be reading, but you yourself will be coming to heaven with each post that Matthew does.

Matthew:

I am without words. I am shocked. I wonder how many people will see you now?

John the Baptist:

The Bible says that as a believer, you are seated in heavenly places. Why not read these accounts and take a seat in the room each time you read? Next to me, as you look at me on my right, which is your left, is Elijah. He is dressed in orange like a Buddhist monk dresses. He also has a white turban as does everyone in the room, even you, Matthew. The meaning of those might be disclosed later.

Elijah:

It's good to see you here today. You are getting thirsty down on earth, so you are going to make a coffee. I will be here, ready to speak once you have prepared it.

Wow, that is a nice coffee made with milk. I just had a sip.

Matthew, I don't want you or your readers to be confused.

You are special to be here and recording these conversations. You were destined to do this all your life. Many thousands of people will be blessed by this. You have the special skill set and the special faith to do this as well as an understanding editor. So you have been especially selected for this task.

The point we want to make to your readers is that you are not so special that they, too, can't have the same experience. I want everyone reading this to know that they, too, can learn to come to heaven.

(Elijah takes a few grapes and puts them in his mouth.)

I speak through my mind to Matthew so that I can chew and speak at the same time. Can you see me smiling and chewing? I have a broad smile. Can you see me? If you can, stay in the room as more people speak.

To my right is Enoch. He is in royal blue with his white turban. He is clean shaven and is waving at this moment.

Enoch:

Saints, it is wonderful to speak to you. In the years to come, according to the prophecy in the Bible in Revelation 11, I am going to come to earth. At that time, Elijah and I are going to bring the world into line and prepare her for the Lord's second coming.

I hope that before then, you might find out more about me.

What you might first know about me is that I am a lover of God. I am a person whose heart cannot beat without God. Yes, that is right. I have a heart and a body of flesh here in heaven. God is everything to me, and his son Jesus is just as precious to me.

What I feel that you should all do is to pursue Jesus with all your heart. If you make a concerted effort into drawing close to Jesus, you will be able to cope if you are alive on earth during the tribulation. That is the good news I have to share with you right now. Don't fear the end of days.

To my right is Moses. He is in royal blue with his white turban. He is my twin, ha ha. Now, he has a larger girth than me. He has what they call a barrel chest but not from drinking a lot of beer. He is simply a big man.

Moses:

Hi, Matthew.

Matthew:

I have met you before in my house. It is good to see you again.

Moses:

I have a calling for you similar to mine. You relate very much to me because the church, by and large, is under the slavery of the world and its lusts. Very few people live a life set apart. The church operates at a much lower level than what it could be. You are called to bring the world out of slavery from the almighty dollar.

I am going to work with you as well as with most of these saints in this room. Long after the series of books is finished, I will work with you. I am going to work with your heart. I am going to teach you how to be a leader over millions. I am going to teach you how to manage a large group of people.

I will be your friend and minister to you. I will show you what you need to say to my people. I will teach you how to be a spokesman for the Almighty.

Matthew:

Woah! That is huge. I felt sad that you led the people for 40 years and then became sad and angry and didn't enter the Promised Land. I was sad for you. I hope I don't become disqualified because I get frustrated.

Moses:

That is sweet, Matthew. I went into the Promised Land when I appeared to Jesus on the Mount of Transfiguration. That was an exciting day for me. I am going to visit earth quite a lot in the future. I had to give the leadership to Joshua at some time. I don't have regrets. What a mighty Lord we serve! I praise God that we can speak. Yes, you saw me come to your kitchen as we spoke. Yes, I guess like you, we can be in two places at once.

Bob:

How is that jacket feeling now, Matthew? You were quite relaxed during this trip. We have covered enough for today and this post. Say goodbye to the room.

(Matthew arrives back on earth.)

See how easy that is? You don't need to worry.

Matthew:

I had no idea that starting these conversations with you would end with me going to heaven each time.

Bob:

That is the Lord you serve. He is full of surprises. Have a good night. Goodbye.

Matthew:

Bye, Bob

Message 10

Bob:

How are you, now?

Matthew:

I was lying down to go to sleep but could not rest. I am so excited about heaven. I have three friends, Anna, June and Niels, who are reading each post and are just as excited by each of them as I am. It is not only so much fun to go to heaven, but it is also exciting to hear my friends are reading my posts and seeing heaven also. It is so good. It fills my heart with joy that people will not only read these accounts, learn from the saints and Jesus but also have encounters of their own.

I hope that they linger in heaven like June did and have their own conversations with the saints. I am just so happy. I can see these books going on for many years. I can see some people just reading and reading all the way through.

Bob:

We really have you excited. Now, it's time to ascend. Are you ready?

Matthew:

Sure am!

Bob:

Okay, here we are. Today, we have a council table of 13 seats with a round table. No head place is assigned as we are all equal. Today, we are going to have a good time. Matthew was telling Jesus that he is so excited, and he can see these books going for a quite a while.

Jesus:

"My Visits to the Galactic Council of Heaven" sounds like a good title. You can name your blog posts that from now on. I am so excited to have you come here each day. The bug has bitten you. We have you hooked, and now, like drinking coffee, this will become natural to you. I want this to be normal.

Just so that people aren't freaked out, 12 people and you are here like my 12 disciples with me. We are going to invite others into the room from time to time. The Holy Spirit will direct who visits. We'll stay with the core group of 13, but we will have others come from time to time.

How does that sound?

Matthew:

That sounds awesome. I think that I heard the first name in my spirit. Was that who I thought it was?

Jesus:

Yes, it was your grandmother, Grace. Here she is.

Grace:

(Grace is in what looks like a freshly pressed white gown and is smiling brightly at me and seems a little nervous to speak.)

Hello, Matthew. It is so good to see you here. I have seen you come to this room the last few times you have been here. All of heaven is watching this from their TV sets, where they can watch anything they like. We all have something like TVs in heaven, and we can tune them into any saint we are interested in and watch what they are doing. I can tell you that there is much excitement in what you are doing. So many saints want to speak to you.

People stop me when I am walking through heaven and say, "You are Matthew's grandmother. It is so good to meet you."

Believe me. Your friend, Harry, said that you have a coffee shop named after you up here. Heaven has a chain of them, and people go to have a coffee or a drink there, and they pray for you. You thought that was a bit weird, yet it is true. The coffee shops are everywhere, and everyone knows who you are up here.

People who are reading this might have a hard time believing it. And yes, you are having a hard time typing it due to your humility. But time will tell, and one day, the people of the world will know why you are so loved up here.

You have a friend, Laura, that says you shine like Jesus up here. You struggled believing that. I have to tell you that you really do shine like him. You are often walking through heaven without even being conscious of it, and people just stop and stare at you. Laura told you that, and you were shocked. I can tell you, as your grandmother who loves you, that this is true.

You remember the other day when you were at the Crystal Sea, and you noticed everyone looking at you and listening to what you were saying. That is the effect that you have when you are in heaven. The people here are fascinated with you. I am just so happy that I have the chance to say hello to you.

You noticed I was nervous to speak to you. It was not that I was nervous to speak to the grandson whom I loved when you were growing up. The reason I was nervous was because the glory that is coming off your face is really amazing. I have trouble understanding how you have become who you are. I have been watching you. I have watched your whole life and seen everything you went through. I know how close you are to Jesus. And now I see you in all your glory. I am just so happy.

Matthew:

You are right. It was hard for me to type that. I am glad that my three friends that are reading this love me. I am sure some of the future readers will have put the books down by now. I don't understand why I have so much glory, but I have had enough prophecies and prophetic people speak about it that I have to just accept it by faith.

I know that you would not lie to me. I know that they brought you in to say that to me. I know that you love me. I wondered how I was going to interview all the saints in heaven that wanted to speak to me. I guess we are going to do a lot of that in this room.

Did I hear correctly when I was washing dishes in the kitchen that time? Is my mother's father also here in heaven?

Grace:

Yes, he is here in heaven. One day, your mother will meet him. She cannot accept that now, but she will be reunited with him when she comes here in the future.

Bob:

The Father wanted you to meet Grace right now. She will be watching everything and listening to what goes on. She is right — heaven is tuning into this. You cannot receive it now, and you will take a while to come to grips with it, but even as Bob Jones, it is more of an honor for me to be in your company then for you to be in mine. Grace will visit in the future to steady you as we go on.

Matthew:

Bye, Grace.

Grace:

Bye, my love. Be good.

Jesus:

Okay, Matthew. How was that?

Matthew:

It was a bit embarrassing to have that said about me. I guess that is what you wanted said, and it has its purpose. It is amazing to know that heaven is tuning in. It is a great thought that people want to speak to Grace and that she is popular up here because of me. I am so happy that my mother's dad is here.

Jesus:

You don't even know his name. That is him sitting over there. You can see him waving.

(The room suddenly expanded, and we were not just in a room with a round table, but now we were in an arena similar to a mega church with the table and chairs in the middle and thousands of people surrounding us, sitting and watching. In the first row of seats, next to where Grace sat down, was my grandfather. They had front row seats.)

Matthew:

I was in this room about 20 years ago. I was talking to some saints, and about 10,000 people sitting in chairs were all around watching. And here I am now. It's amazing. I am overcome because rather than watching TV sets, these people are watching in this arena.

Jesus:

I love watching your face. You have been meditating on Ephesians 3:20 for three years now, Matthew. Would this be that type of moment for you?

"Now to Him who is able to do exceedingly abundantly above all that we ask or think, according to the power that works in us"

Matthew:

Yes, this is definitely this verse coming true in my life. I am blown away. When I saw the arena 20 years ago, I didn't know it was this huge. I am amazed. I can hear names of some of those that are in the front rows.

John Paul Jackson:

I have not met all of these people yet, Matthew. I have met a lot of saints, but every single saint of any repute is in this room. Thousands of them are here, and they would all like to hear what is going on. And many of them will come down and join us.

I am overcome that I am even at this table. I am so humbled to be here. I honestly can't stop crying. I am undone.

I want you to know that you are here for a good reason. I want you to know that you are simply doing what you are called to do. The good thing about you not having a lot of friends is that people won't tell you not to do this. The good thing about not having a big ministry is that you can take risky steps like this.

I have watched your life. I have watched every time you saw a prostitute. I have seen you search far and wide for love. I have heard you cry. I have seen you do things for Jesus that few people would do. I have sat down with God and Jesus while they showed me the best things that you have done on earth. Jesus and the Father were showing you off to me and showing me why you were so special to them.

I saw you in the pool, doing dive bombs because Jesus told you to do it. I saw you give a street-walking prostitute $100.00 because Jesus set you up to have a divine encounter with her in that part of the city.

I saw you eat McDonald's with a homeless man who everyone else thought was weird.

I saw you go through hundreds of tests.

I saw you feed the homeless and give them drinks. I saw you invite the homeless to live in your house three times. I saw you go to a psychiatric ward to visit a sick man when you could have been locked up yourself. I saw you give love to the people that were unlovable in the world's eyes.

Jesus and the Father have all these things put to music. You are a model of the parable of the sheep and the goats. You are Jesus on earth.

Oh, yes, people will look at you and say he is nothing great. People will read this and think that they are better then you. But most of what you have done has not been seen by anyone but the people involved.

God wants you to speak to the people. God wants you to serve as a model for others. You enjoy quoting Paul when he said, "Imitate me as I imitate Christ." You know that was quite a statement.

God wants the world to imitate you. You are a model.

I know that you don't know me. I know you only watched a couple of videos of mine. But you know truth when it is said. You can feel my love. You know that the Father has a film or show reel with the highlights of all the best events in your life to be seen by others in heaven.

Do you know that we have every single prophetic encounter that you have had with strangers? Do you know I have watched every one of them? Do you know I was so impressed? Then, you wrote a book showing people how to do it.

I am so humbled to know you.

Yes, I had a platform, and I had a great name among men. But, I have seen you at your worst, and even then, you were a good guy.

Before I go I just want to tell you, Anna, that you are precious to Matthew and to Jesus. We love you because you have childlike faith, and you have heaps of love and compassion. You are a gentle soul, and we love you and the light that you bring to the world. Keep on being you and surrendering to the Holy Spirit because you are doing a good job.

Jesus:

How are you feeling now?

Matthew:

It seems today is all about me. I am amazed that you have that show reel in heaven with all those good things that I have done. I guess you have a lot of encounters filmed that I have had with the homeless there. I am blown away that you can do that. The fact that you can show people all the best parts of my life surprises me.

I knew that you had saved all of my encounters that I have had with strangers using prophetic evangelism. I hope that you can have an angel deliver that to earth some time so that I can use it to teach people. It would be really cool to have that footage.

Jesus:

We could do that one day. But wouldn't it be cool for you to have your own footage one day with hidden cameras or some other way? That is a surprising thing about you. You are not interested in looking good. You are only interested in equipping people to be like you.

It must have been a shock for you to hear John Paul Jackson say that people should imitate you.

Matthew:

Yes, it was. I have thought about saying that in the future and am almost thinking of writing a book about that one day. I was surprised to hear him say that about me.

If I watched the videos of my life, I know I would have a much better opinion of myself than I currently do.

Isaiah:

The glory of the Lord is all over you, Matthew. You just don't see it; that is all. But when you come here, your whole soul and spirit shines. It is so bright, isn't it, folks?

(The whole auditorium gets to their feet and claps.)

Matthew:

I am overcome. I guess in heaven, I seem like a Benny Hinn or a Joyce Meyer.

Jesus:

You just keep being you, Matthew. Keep coming here when you have the chance. Some people have the "travel bug." You are going to get the "heaven encounters bug."

Peter:

You are a great guy, Matthew. It is hard not to feel overwhelmed with all that is happening. It must have been amazing to see all these people rise to their feet and clap for you. You are a hero up here. We know who you are. In time, earth will come to see who you are.

Elijah:

I told you three weeks ago that I won't be on earth for at least 20 years. You have all that time. You might not be well known now, but in 20 years, you'll be well known. Just keep putting one foot in front of the other. Keep doing what the Holy Spirit says to do.

That is all people should be doing. Everyone that knows the Lord should be following the Holy Spirit. People should receive their direction and assignments from him.

I know that might seem foreign to some, but I don't know how people cope without direction from God.

They honor God with their mouths, but their hearts are far from him.

A time will come to earth in the future where you will have to be able to hear from the Holy Spirit and receive directions from him. A time will come when your life will be in danger if you can't hear the Holy Spirit.

I guess we will speak more on that at another time.

How cool is it that you have all these people in this room to talk to?

Matthew:

It is cool all right. I have not even spoken to all of you yet. It was great to see my grandmother and hear what she had to say to me today. I look forward to every visit that I am going to make.

Paul:

Don't think about what is said. Don't go and check it for theology. Don't worry about what we say about you. Don't worry about what people might say. Don't worry. Worry isn't welcome in heaven, and if you worry, you affect the flow.

Your grandmother was nervous, and yes, it was because of your glory and who you have become. However, she was also nervous about what she would say and put out there for your readers to read.

People might expect us to be perfect up here, but we have emotions and feelings. We care for you.

The best way you are going to get through this is to just relax. Don't try and consider what we are saying and how it will sound. Instead, simply type and say what we are saying. Things will go well that way. Don't freak out. Just put our words out there.

It has been 2,000 years, and people are still debating what I have said. God knows, people are still in fierce debate about what John wrote in Revelation. All you can do as a prophet is come up here, talk to us, type what you hear and assemble it into a readable format with your editor and release it.

God knows what he is doing. The Holy Spirit knows what he is doing. We all know what we are doing. Be a little like me. Be bold and courageous and write and let the words fall where they may on the hearts of the readers.

I love you, and I am proud of you. It is time for you to go.

Matthew:

Bye, Paul. Thanks for that. It's hard to leave.

Bob:

Come on, Matthew. It is time to go.

Matthew:

Thanks.

Bob:

Now fix the typos and post this. Have a good day. Why don't you stay up and go and visit your shopping center on the bus?

Matthew:

I will. Thanks for starting this, Bob.

Bob:

I was just being led by God as you are. I am proud of you. This is really out there. Few men would have the courage to do this. You will be rewarded one day for this. See you later!

Message 11

Bob:

Hi, Matthew. How are you?

Matthew:

I slept well and feel rested. I have had some attacks from the enemy over these encounters. Other than that, I am pretty good.

Bob:

Ready to go?

Matthew:

Yes. Wow! I am here already.

(Jesus has tears in his eyes again. He is hugging me and showing me to the table. He waves his hand to show me the audience and has me take my seat.)

Jesus:

It is only natural that satan would attack you through your mind, Matthew. He is questioning you about the point of all of this. He is challenging the benefit for the readers.

Matthew:

Yes. That is what he is asking through my thoughts.

Jesus:

What could be harmful about you seeing me each day so that we could get to know each other better? What would be boring about people of the faith speaking to you each day? The enemy is just scared. We have had thousands of conversations in the past. You could ask what is the point of those conversations if you can't even remember what we discussed. The point of them is that we have a wonderful relationship now, grounded in love and experience. I have been with you through thick and thin.

The saints want to do life with you. They want to grow close to you. You are going to be refreshed by what they say, and you are going to grow in your love for them and your faith in me through it all. The readers will keep reading as they learn more and more about the saints, about their faith and about everything that they talk about.

Satan's lies always contain an element of truth. Something in them always hurts. The very fact that he is attacking you is all the more the reason to proceed.

Matthew:

Why were you crying?

Jesus:

I know how you were feeling. I know you were under attack. I know if we didn't start this, you would not have been attacked in this way. I love you, Matthew. I don't like it when you are under attack. They were tears of compassion. I love you so much. The hard thing about the spiritual life is that it is a war, and people get hurt.

Matthew:

I am feeling better now.

(Jesus reaches out and hugs me. The whole table of 12 get up and motion for me to hug them all. I go around one by one and hug each one. Each of them tells me that they love me as they pull me close.)

Bob:

You are a champion, Matthew, just like June, your friend, says. Do you know that this is way out there? Nothing has been written in this format before. You are a forerunner. We want all of your readers to become hungry for heaven and encounters so that they want some of their own. We want to open up a gate to heaven through this book. I am so proud of you. We knew that your attack was coming, and we couldn't tell you about it. You had to weather it by yourself and overcome.

People have authority to help others in the areas that they overcome by faith. God in his wisdom allows people to suffer and go through trials, not for the sake of the suffering but for the sake of redemption. For instance, you had a long battle with prostitutes. You were addicted for years. Then, you overcame it and broke free. Your testimony now has power over other people who have had the same struggle.

More recently, you went through deliverance and broke free of a pornography addiction that you have had all your life. You tried everything to break free, and now, you are free. Soon, you will write a book about your struggle and everything you tried, and you will end the book with the website of the man that ministered to you so that other people can seek him out. If you had not struggled for as many years as you had, your story would not be as powerful. You feel on top of the world and so free. You have great faith in this deliverance minister now. You know that anyone that wants to break free should try him out.

His information can be found at
http://www.freedomencounters.com/

You have had these two main struggles. However, you have struggled with many other things in your life. The struggles and the suffering are what make you such a powerful person in the Kingdom. The fact that you had struggles does not disqualify you but rather qualifies you to speak on these subjects — just the opposite of what you would expect.

You had a recent struggle this morning with satan opposing you coming here. This will bear fruit. People who read this will see that if they are going to ascend and meet with Jesus and saints in heaven, and if they make a practice of it, then they will also encounter opposition. They will also learn to run to Jesus and let him walk them through it until they are comfortable with the process.

So you see, struggles are a part of life, yet through overcoming them, we clear out a path that can help other people who encounter the same struggles later. You are loved so much. You see, we did not warn you as you needed to have the full impact of the battle so that your testimony was secure and helpful to others.

Matthew:

I see that now. Well, all of my issues are out there now. I have to laugh. Things have their own way of happening when I am up here. If I were choosing what should be said up here, half the conversations wouldn't happen. When Grace, my grandmother, said those great things about me, I wanted to hide. But now here you are, telling everyone about my sexual struggles, and once again, I am cringing. I guess there is balance in my account now. If they thought that I was high and mighty, they might have changed their minds now and realized that I am a fallen man who is simply lovesick for Jesus.

Paul:

That is why I had to say that I was the greatest sinner, Matthew. People met me and saw my life and thought they could never live up to the life that I was leading. There is wisdom in sharing what you have been through that is distasteful. People have an easier time relating to you if they see that you are a person with issues just like them.

People grab hold of my words and hear that I was the greatest of sinners and assume that I continued to be the greatest of sinners. That is an incorrect assumption. The message of my life was that the grace of God can help you walk in new life. But a new life isn't very powerful if you don't have an old life.

I consider it real wisdom for Bob to share some of your struggles with the readers. The last thing that we want people thinking is that you are some great person who is better than everyone else so that they have the opinion that you can come here because you are so special, but because they are ordinary, they can't come.

Sure, you are unique. It is that true you are very special to Jesus, and everyone in heaven knows who you are. It was true what Jesus said when the woman washed his feet with her tears. He said that one that has been forgiven much actually loves much. It is true that you have stood out as a saint that is really someone special.

But even so, you only love so much because you have been through so much.

The Christian life can be treated with disdain and with a lack of respect. Many people don't put their whole heart into their walk with God. Many people just coast along, and Jesus doesn't seem to be too important to them. Not many Christians walk with Jesus as their very breath with the world holding no allure for them. Many Christians love the world and all it has to offer and therefore, don't ever become as zealous as you. In that way, you are a special breed. You have nothing to live for outside of God's will for your life. You have no job; you are on a pension, so you have no life outside of writing your books and giving personal prophecies to people. You don't have any interest in living like the world does.

The people of God need to realize that fancy clothes, fancy cars, fancy I-phones and Apple products and other expensive possessions don't buy you favor with God. The idea that you have to have more and more is a snare — a very crafty one that satan uses. I said this very clearly in Scripture.

We should not get caught up with the things of the world. 2 Timothy 2:3-4 says this: "You therefore must endure hardship as a good soldier of Jesus Christ. No one engaged in warfare entangles himself with the affairs of this life, that he may please him who enlisted him as a soldier."

The average Christian does not think that that they are entangled with the things of this world, but they are. They are addicted to the world and all that it offers them. If that were not so, they would welcome death more easily.

I speak of the love of money being a snare, but it is not just the love of money, it is the love of the world and all that is in it.

1 Timothy 6:6-10:

"Now godliness with contentment is great gain. For we brought nothing into this world, and it is certain we can carry nothing out. And having food and clothing, with these we shall be content. But those who desire to be rich fall into temptation and a snare, and into many foolish and harmful lusts which drown men in destruction and perdition. For the love of money is a root of all kinds of evil, for which some have strayed from the faith in their greediness, and pierced themselves through with many sorrows."

Many people read the above Scripture passage, Matthew, and they say to themselves that they are not in love with money, so they think that I am not speaking about them.

But sadly, few people understand that the world and all its desires takes money to accumulate. I am surprised at how selfish the Christian church has become nowadays.

What I love about you, my friend, is that you have a love for God and his will above all else in the world. Sure, you live in the world, and that requires money, but you get by with less than many others so that you can invest the majority of your money into writing and publishing your books. It's funny that so many people ask why you sell most of your books for 99 cents, and they can't seem to grasp that you would simply give them away if Amazon let you do that. People cannot understand why you would spend thousands of dollars to produce books, only to give them away or sell them so cheaply. These people are thinking of worldly ways and not godly ways.

Matthew:

Yes, I have to explain that a lot. People don't seem to understand when I share the reason with them that I want to make my books inexpensive so that money doesn't stop others from buying them.

I don't think I will ever raise the price on my books. As long as God supplies me with the money to produce books, they will be the cheapest that I can make them. I even went to the effort to make one of my best books permanently free on Amazon, and a couple of hundred people download it each month.

Paul:

It is so good to talk to you and your readers. I have really come to love you over the years. I have watched you all of your life. I have known all along that I was going to be meeting you in these encounters. I knew that this would happen. I am so excited to speak to you.

I know that, for the most part, you find my writing in the Bible hard to follow. I would prefer that you are honest instead of pretending that you understand it and going along with what other people say about the Scriptures.

I know that you admire me for the suffering that I went through and the fact that I was so bold.

Every time you slept with a prostitute and walked out feeling worthless and condemned, I cried for you. I have wept so many tears over your life. All those tens of thousands of dollars you spent to be touched, to be listened to, to connect with a woman, all of those dollars you spent trying to connect with love, ripped my heart to pieces. But you went on and on, drowning in this world that doesn't seem to love you. All of heaven watched you. We were all watching everything.

And now, here you are, speaking to us. And here we are, speaking to you. And now, I have the chance to speak with you face to face. I am so happy that you have overcome. I am happier still with the person that you have become. You are a soldier that does not entangle yourself with the affairs of this world any longer.

Jesus said that we cannot serve two masters. He said we will end up loving one and despising the other if we try. Then, he went on to say that we can't love God while we love money and possessions. The problem with the church is that they love their money and possessions, and they secretly despise God even though they praise him. This is why churches preach that you can have expensive cars and houses and all the riches that you want and still serve God. They preach a message that is very appealing, but the Word still applies whether they know it or not. Many of those wealthy Christians who live lavish lifestyles don't have rich relationships with God. They might say that they do. But Jesus' words don't lie.

Of course, you can be wealthy and have all the best the world can offer and have a passionate love affair with Jesus if you are giving much of your wealth to the poor and to God. I wrote about that also in 1 Timothy 6:17-19: "Command those who are rich in this present age not to be haughty, nor to trust in uncertain riches but in the living God, who gives us richly all things to enjoy. Let them do good, that they be rich in good works, ready to give, willing to share, storing up for themselves a good foundation for the time to come, that they may lay hold on eternal life."

In this way, you can have the best that the world can offer and also be in the will of God and not loving the world and its lusts, but few people ever achieve that balance in their life.

God knows your attitude toward money, Matthew, so he is confident that he can pour money and blessings into your ministry, and you will only ever spend the money on him and his ministry in your life. We need to speak to you at length here in your visits so that people have an idea of who you are and how you live so that your readers can also begin to live that way.

It is time for you to go now. I wish you goodbye. Give me a hug.

Matthew:

Thanks, Paul. It was so refreshing to hear from you. Thanks for the hug.

Bob:

Come on, brother.

Matthew:

I don't want to go.

Jesus:

You can come any time you choose. We have to look out for your readers and not give them too much to process at once. We'll see you later on. Bye now.

Matthew:

Bye, Bob. (I found myself back on earth.)

Bob:

Bye, Matthew.

Message 12

Bob:

Hi, Matthew. How are you today?

Matthew:

I am feeling a bit weird. I was sick yesterday and slept a lot. Today, I have a funny feeling. I don't feel like doing anything. I wish I could sleep, but I have slept too much. Here you are saying, "Let's go to heaven," so I have put on some worship music, taken out my computer, and I am ready.

Bob:

Let us ascend.

Jesus:

(Jesus greets me with a hug as I enter the council.)

Welcome, Matthew. We have missed you for a couple of days. I know that the enemy has been attacking you and making you think that this is stupid and a waste of your time. I want you to know that, as sure as I am seated here, smiling at you and the other 11 people here, and the stadium is full of people, that this is real and important. What we say to you is important for you to know. What we say is important for your readers to read.

You are facing opposition because this is worthwhile. The opposition is not because this book is hopeless. Give me a big smile. That's right. Soon enough, we will be into this session, and you will be in the anointing and warmed up.

Matthew:

Thanks, Jesus. I still wonder at all of this. Yes, I have been attacked. I might not be in the mood, but Bob turned up and told me to come. It feels good to smile.

Bob:

You are a champion, Matthew. It is good that you move forward even when you don't feel like it. You have dedication and purpose. I am so proud of you. You were not in a good place yesterday, and it is so good that you can get up and do this today. Do you know that the saints in the Word did not minister out of their strengths all the time? Paul shared that he ministered out of his weaknesses and brought God glory. It is what you do on your hard days that makes a difference. Anyone can do great things on their good days. It's what you do with your mediocre days that sets you apart.

Of course, I never had bad days on earth!

Matthew:

You're funny.

Bob:

Today, we are going to have a bit of a different day. Today, some of the saints are going to ask you a question. I want you to answer, not only for the saint to hear the answer, but for the readers to learn a bit more about you. You have talked with some of them before but not with all of them. Here is the first saint.

Malachi:

You know I wrote about a man treating the wife of his youth wrongly. Do you think you have healed from your marriage?

Matthew:

This makes me emotional. I have tried to heal from my marriage break up. But sometimes, I still feel anger toward my former wife. Do you know that I am sick and tired of all the counseling that I have had? I wish everything could just be healed in one go without dredging up the same things again and again.

No, I am not healed.

Malachi:

I think you might look into some healing, my son. I am sorry to bring up this painful topic. I know that you like to read parts of my book. Do you know that we have a book of remembrance about your life? Malachi 3:16 talks about this: "Then those who feared the Lord spoke to one another, And the Lord listened and heard them; So a book of remembrance was written before Him For those who fear the Lord And who meditate on His name."

I have your book before me here.

(He lifts it up and shows me.)

As you read through it, it plays videos of your life and replays your conversations. Do you know you speak about the Lord Jesus quite often, my son?

Matthew:

Yes, I do. Sometimes, I wish I had more people I could talk to.

Malachi:

Get some of your hurts healed, mate.

Peter:

You admire the fact that I asked Jesus the most questions and was always the first to try and answer his questions. You were happy when the Holy Spirit told you that. Do you like that about yourself the most?

Matthew:

Yes, I am hungry. I always have questions. I really like that I am like you in that regard. I am the most outspoken in any learning situation. I like that about you more than the fact that you used to heal thousands with your shadow, even though I would like to do that as well.

I have so much love for you, Peter. I think you have been largely mispresented by many pastors who don't know who you really are and just share what is written about you in the Word. I guess I love you because I am so misunderstood as well.

Peter:

That is also true, my friend. You are way out there. The Holy Spirit makes it really easy for others to misunderstand you. Yet the Holy Spirit is after the radical and passionate ones, and that is who you manage to reach. You are a pure vessel. You are so radical and obedient. Heaven loves you for that because we know we can tell you anything, and you will say it. You have so much faith in God and his ways. Because we have more capacity in our hearts to love in heaven, I want you to know that I love you **more** than you love me. I honor you, my friend.

Matthew:

Now you have me crying.

Peter:

Heaven cries with you, my beloved.

Moses:

Hello, Matthew. I know that you look at my life, and you don't focus on the signs and wonders that I did. You have faith that you could do the same if you were sent. Your focus is on the people of God and how they complained in the wilderness and wanted to go back to Egypt.

Why do you want to bring the people of earth out of their Egypt?

Matthew:

Because there is so much joy and fulfillment in doing the will of God. The first thing is that the people of God don't even know that they are in slavery to the world and its lusts. They are in bondage, and they don't even know it.

I guess I want to wake up the people and show them that they were created with a purpose and a destiny and lead them to it. I feel the world is not going to be impacted in any great way until they have come out of their Egypt.

Moses:

So you want the church to be free so that they can lead the world to true freedom?

Matthew:

Yes, that is right. I want the church to become relevant and proactive in reaching the lost. The church can't seem to make a big impact yet because they are asleep and in slavery to the world. Revelation 3:1 puts it this way: "And to the angel of the church in Sardis write, 'These things says He who has the seven Spirits of God and the seven stars: 'I know your works, that you have a name that you are alive, but you are dead.' "

I love the church; I love people, but with all the teaching and books in the world, people don't seem to be learning how to be alive and don't know how to run a church that is alive and relevant. And according to this Scripture, the churches that people think are alive are actually dead. It makes me sad. I am glad you are here to be with me in the years to come.

Moses:

It will be my pleasure to be with you. See you.

John the Apostle:

Do you think it is possible to walk and live like Jesus did?

Matthew:

Yes, I believe that it is. You wrote the same in your epistle. I have never heard a pastor preach on it. 1 John 2:6 tell us, "He who says he abides in Him ought himself also to walk just as He walked."

This verse not only says that we can walk and act like Jesus, it says that as the author of this verse, you walked this way. Just because it is not preached in churches, doesn't mean that it can't be done.

I feel that a person can live to become what David and Jeremiah spoke of. Psalm 1:3 says, "He shall be like a tree planted by the rivers of water, that brings forth its fruit in its season, whose leaf also shall not wither; and whatever he does shall prosper."

Jeremiah 17:7-8 states,

"Blessed *is* the man who trusts in the Lord, and whose hope is the Lord. For he shall be like a tree planted by the waters, which spreads out its roots by the river, and will not fear when heat comes; but its leaf will be green, and will not be anxious in the year of drought, nor will cease from yielding fruit."

We are not only to trust in the Lord, but we are to become trees that bear fruit and provide sustenance to everyone who needs it that comes to us. We are not meant to be selfish, world-loving Christians, but we are meant to be a source of comfort and answers for this desperate world.

John the Apostle:

I see that I have brought up some of your life verses that you live by. You do a good job, Matthew. It was great to talk to you.

Elijah:

Are you prepared for the future?

Matthew:

I have learned to live by being guided by the Holy Spirit. I personally believe that I can survive anything that the Lord wants me to survive simply by taking directions from him. The Holy Spirit knows how to guide me, so I am confident in my future with him by my side.

Elijah:

Do you know that not many Christians could answer that way?

Matthew:

Yes, it is sad that they can't answer that way. Many Christians don't know how to hear the Holy Spirit nor do they have a trustworthy relationship built with him. One of the most important things a Christian should learn is how to hear God through each person of the Trinity. A person should be able to hear from God the Father, Jesus and the Holy Spirit. In the future, their life will depend on it. In years to come, individual pastors will not be able to lead them and their family to safety.

I know one day I have to write a book on how to hear from God. Some good books are out there on this topic, and I have not worked out how I will write it, but I can see the need for it.

Enoch:

Do you know the secret to the higher things in the Kingdom?

Matthew:

I feel that it is personal intimacy. I feel that when we have our relationship with God right, then he can show us anything. I feel that my intimacy with Jesus allows these visits to happen. I read the book of Enoch once, and I have to say that it was all above my head, but the one thing I know is that God loved you so much and liked being around you so much that he brought you home early.

God has told me that he would like to bring me home early also, yet I have a job to do on earth that is more important. That is why I have no fear of death. I am happy to go home anytime, but I know I will be here right to the end. I know you will be here also one day. I look forward to seeing what you do on earth.

Enoch:

I look forward to spending time with you when I come.

Paul:

What do you think is your biggest strength?

Matthew:

My love. I have learned to love people like God loves them. I have learned to have compassion and to love. It is the love I have for other people that compels me to write and publish this book. It is my love for God that compels me to write about the hard things and the meat that many people are not talking about. I love people too much to be silent. Though I am lonely at times, I have a lot of love in me for people.

Paul:

Great answer, my friend. The Christian faith is nothing but love. You love well. I look forward to you getting to know me better through your visits.

John Paul Jackson:

If you could pick one of your books to sell millions of copies, which one would it be?

Matthew:

I think the book I am going to write on the commandments of Jesus would be the one that I would like to sell millions of copies. Whether people would start to obey the commands would be another thing. Do you think they would obey?

John Paul Jackson:

In order to obey, people need to crucify their flesh. The flesh is very important to many people and wields a lot of power in many Christians' lives. It will be a good book for you to write. The people who are meant to be changed will be changed by it.

I love how you are so intense. That puts off a lot of people. They don't understand you. But you are so focused on the Kingdom. I can't wait till you are given a world stage. You are going to do such a good job. When that happens, you won't have to fear; you will have a group of supportive people around you.

You will meet some exciting people on earth and work with them. These are people that will think like you and that will be good for you. I love you, my friend, please come up here as often as you can. I have much to say to you.

Bob:

What could heaven do for you?

Matthew:

Have my angel, Mark, find readers that would support me each month so that I can increase the number of books that I release.

Bob:

You are funny. You are all about the Kingdom. Yes, we will work on that for you. Many people would have asked for other things. But you seem to know that the more books you have, the more people can be educated.

Jesus:

That was a great answer. We will work on that. Well, it is time for us to wrap up. I hope that people got to know you better through this. I want you to know that I am very happy with you. I am so glad that you pushed through today and made the effort to connect with us. It was hard going at first, but you made it and gave some great answers. You do love well. Bye for now.

Matthew:

Bye, saints.

Bob:

I think it would be good for you to go shopping today and pay your bills. You need to get out.

Matthew:

Thanks, Bob. I will do that. Bye for now.

Message 13

Bob:

Hello, Matthew. How are you?

Matthew:

I am okay. I couldn't sleep, so I got up a couple of hours ago. Here I am now, ready for my next adventure.

Bob:

Shall we ascend?

Matthew:

Let's go.

(Here we are. Jesus hugs me.)

Hi, my friend

Jesus:

You are looking good. It is good to see you. I am so pleased that you come each day, and you are not letting the attacks stop you. I love you so much. You have been through so much in your life. I bet you never guessed that you would be doing this often.

Matthew:

I knew that many people in heaven wanted to be interviewed, and I thought I might interview some of them, but I didn't know that I was going to be here in this arena with them surrounding me like this. An author mentioned Madame Guyon the other day, and she came and saw me. I know that she really touched my life with her book. I like the idea that I can be here and speak to anyone.

Jesus:

Many people reading don't know who Madame Guyon (1648 to 1717) is. She was a Catholic lady who wrote the book, "Experiencing the Depths of Jesus Christ," in which she talked about cultivating intimacy with me, and she taught Matthew how to have two-way conversations with me. Here she is.

Madame Guyon:

Hello, Matthew. It is so good to see you here. I am overcome with love for you. I have watched you and seen your life play out. You are a treasure. Even if you never grew in fame and if you never became popular in Christian circles, your books impact people greatly.

It's good to have dreams and have things to look forward to in life, but you can't live your life for tomorrow and what tomorrow might bring. You have to enjoy each day. You have to have peace and joy each day that you live. You cannot be living in a way that says, "When ______________ happens, then I will be happy." You need to be happy now. People need you to be happy now.

Matthew:

You have a great point. Each day, I look at the numbers of how many people have bought my books and at how many people have downloaded the latest book that I have made free. I receive great joy from knowing that people are being blessed. I guess I wish that more people were downloading them.

How do you remain content?

Madame Guyon:

You have to understand that if you are led by the Spirit of God in all that you say and do, then the Lord has you where he wants you to be. You have to learn to be content in all things.

Some people are reading this and saying to themselves that you have a good life. You get to come here to this place and speak to any saint that you want. Many of them might wonder why you are not content.

You have to look at your life and sometimes, take an inventory of where you are. You have a pretty good life, and you are really blessed. You know that one day in the future, you will be more well-known, and more people will be buying your books.

It is time to be content with who you are and with where you are. Anything less means that you are striving, which means you are not at rest.

Matthew:

You are right. You would understand contentment. You suffered quite a lot. You would know how to receive your joy from God.

Madame Guyon:

You do well. It's just a little striving on your part. You are mostly at rest. You do a good job with your life. It is pretty neat that you can come up here to meet us, isn't it?

Matthew:

I could have never guessed that this was going to happen to me. It still amazes me every time I come here. I am so shocked that Jesus has arranged this. I knew that meeting Bob was big enough for me and hearing that he is going to mentor me was surprising to me, but being given free access to this meeting place and this arena is simply on another level.

Madame Guyon:

You are officially a mystic. People say that I was a mystic. If mystic means that you were very close to Jesus and speaking back and forth to him all the time, yes, that was me.

Jesus is something else. He loves me so much. I delight in him, and we are all one with him up here. Everyone in heaven loves each other, and we are all loved by Jesus. It is so much better being here than being on earth with all its troubles. Even you sense the atmosphere up here every time that you come.

Jesus has wanted you to come to heaven for many years. You never used to come because it hurt so much to go back to earth. Now, you are coming to meet with the council nearly every day. I guess it is different for you now because you can come as often as you like.

Heaven wants people who are reading this to understand that they, too, are welcome to come to heaven. They can come to heaven as they read these accounts and ask any of us questions and hear us speak back to them. We want to interact with the world and all the Christians that are reading.

Well, I have said my piece now. Please look out for me and invite me to your house anytime to catch up. Bye, Matthew.

(Madame Guyon walks away after hugging me and sits down in the arena.)

Moses:

Wow. I guess it was wonderful for you to meet her, right, Matthew?

Matthew:

She holds a special place in my heart, yes. She has touched my life through her book and from all the fruit that came from me being able to hear from Jesus.

Moses:

There is nothing like knowing Jesus. There is nothing that compares to knowing God. I love you so much. Do you know why I love you so much?

Matthew:

That could be for any number of reasons. Is it because I don't give up on Jesus, no matter what I go through?

Moses:

You read my heart. Yes, that is it. You just don't give up. No matter what you suffer, you give praise to Jesus and walk with him wholeheartedly. I love how you also try to learn. I saw you bought the book on reformation, and you can't stand all the talk about apostles and what they do. It pained you to read it, so you had put it down. I love that about you. At least you try to learn. You sought that out because Bob talked to you about how you are going to teach on the coming reformation.

You don't have to worry. Some things are not for you, no matter how keen the people are.

We will teach you what you need to know. We will lead you. We will speak to you. Take my life. How did I go from herding sheep to leading millions of people and being their spiritual father? I learned from the **Lord**. He taught me and gave me the wisdom that I needed to lead them.

So, too, with you. You will be taught by us. We will counsel you. We will show you what you need to know.

Matthew:

Thank you, Moses. Of course, I am sure that you will be able to show me what I need to know. I am just a simple man. I am not that complex. I don't seem to have enough pride about me to be one of these apostles. Where is the humility that I have seen in the apostles that I have met in person? There seems to be so much pride about that office.

Moses:

Pride is not a good thing. I guess in some ways, you are just intimidated by people that speak of power. I have seen you labor though other books, but of late, you don't keep reading once you are bored. It is okay, my friend. You are allowed to be bored with what the author says. We have a way for you.

Matthew:

That is good to know. I am not sure I could be a part of something that thinks they are the answer to the world, no matter how good they are. I just smell pride. I am sorry. Perhaps that is insecurity manifesting in my life.

Moses:

It is a combination of things. You have a good radar for pride. You abhor it just like God does. Of course, you feel you have a better way to share with the church. But you are not saying that your way is the way that people have to go, and if they don't go your way, then they are not rightly aligned. I guess you are a little different as to what you have read and seen.

You are a joy to us. You really please us with all that you do. You don't have to worry about being left behind. You are a key player with a key role in the future of Australia. You just need to be patient for us to open the right doors for you. As Bob said to you before, your message is a little bit strong for the current church, so you need to wait to release it.

You have to consider that I have watched your whole life here in heaven as has the whole arena. We can't tell you your whole future as that would leave you with no room for faith to move forward, but I can assure you that when it comes time for the church to take off, you will be part of it.

I guess that all people wonder what role they will play in their countries. All I can say to people is that you often will get to do what your heart is set on doing for God. Because heaven runs on the Holy Spirit and is free of carnal thoughts, there is no worry up here. Down on earth, you have the worries and concerns that come with life on earth.

I want you to know that you are going to be used in a great way, and you are going to see the world change the way that you want to see it change. You are going to be very happy with what God does in your country and in the U.S. You are going to be a real source of love and comfort for both countries.

You are worried about going to church today. It is okay to miss it if you like. You don't have to be religious about attendance. You have already been to heaven today. You can come up here again later if you choose.

Do you know that you are welcome up here any time that you like? Do you know that Bob will bring you whenever you want to come?

Bob:

That's right, Matthew. I am here for you. You have a good portal in your house. I hope Moses has been putting your mind at rest about the book you were reading and the apostolic network and conference where you were invited. We have many ways to take you, and we will take you the way that best suits your personality.

Matthew:

Thanks, Bob. Thanks, Moses.

Moses:

You have a whole heaven full of friends up here. Everyone wants to talk to you. You are much loved. Don't let worries and fears consume you. Just come up here and see us. It was an honor to speak to you today. I am so glad that you are coming up here. The Lord Jesus has a message for you every time you want to come.

Give my love to Niels, June and Anna, who have been reading these posts. They are good friends to you, Matthew.

Jesus:

I want to tell you Niels that he is in a right place with me. If I came for my Bride now, I would be coming to get him. He does not need to worry about his salvation in the future. I will never let go of him.

I want you to tell June that she is special to me. The way that she has sought me out and pursued me is amazing. I want her to know that I really appreciate who she is.

I want you to tell Anna that she is precious to me. Her giving heart, her love for others and her compassion melt my heart. I love you.

Matthew, you have some amazing friends. I want you to keep them all close. It is time for you to go now.

Matthew:

Bye, Jesus. Bye, all.

(A big 'bye' came from everyone, and they all got on their seats and blew me a kiss.)

Bob:

Feeling better now?

Matthew:

Yes, I have made a decision. It wasn't an easy one and might cost a friendship, but Moses sorted it out. Thanks for today!

Bob

You proofread this and post it now. Bye, Matthew.

Message 14

Bob:

How are you today?

Matthew:

I am happy and really blessed. I can't seem to get over the idea that I can come to heaven each day. I am so happy to go to heaven. I am trying to come to grips with the fact that Jesus allows me to do this.

Bob:

This is because you were born for this. You are going to open the hearts of many to have the same encounters. You are chosen, and you are our special envoy to the earth to show them what is possible. Shall we ascend?

Matthew:

(Jesus has tears in his eyes.)

Why are you crying, Jesus?

Jesus:

I am just overcome with you. I am so happy to see you each day. You fill my eyes with tears of happiness. You are such a joy to me. I am so happy that you have pressed in and have decided to come each day. Do you know that there are certain people that I want to read these books and to seek to come to heaven as well? I want to speak to them, also. I am crying because it is not only such a joy to see you, but I am crying because of the joy set before me of all the people that are going to come after you.

I did not create this world for people to be alone. When I was on earth, I spent a lot of my time up here communing with my Father and angels. Let me share a Scripture with you. John 3:13 tells us, "No one has ascended to heaven but He who came down from heaven, that is, the Son of Man who is in heaven."

You see that when I was on earth, I was still in heaven. It is my wish that I was a forerunner for this. The people of God should be experiencing heaven as often as they wish. You can certainly testify that it is a completely different atmosphere up here.

Matthew:

I certainly can. When I am with you guys, I feel like I am invincible and that I can do anything. Visiting here certainly builds one's faith. I am so overcome with the thoughts that I can do this every day. I am so blessed. I feel so special, yet I know that any person who is saved and who desires this can come. It is just so exciting.

Jesus:

You are opening up a new realm of possibilities for people. People simply need to learn how to see in the Spirit. Michael Van Vlymen and Praying Medic have two good books on the subject. When people learn to see in the Spirit, they will be able to come to heaven, and they can have encounters like you.

People often learn from seeing things. Sometimes, a person has to do something the first time to show others the way and to show them that it can be possible.

Yes, heaven loves you. You are special to us. There is a purpose for you to be here to grow in faith, and not all people are in the same place with us as you are. You will continue to do things first and show people the way, but you are not any more important than any of your readers. You are special, but you are not above anyone. That is hard to align with, but it is the truth.

I love people. I want them here. I have things that I want to teach them. I have things that I want my saints to teach them. I want my people to be encouraged and blessed. I want people to learn. I want my people to move from the ordinary to the extraordinary. I want people to move from the natural to the supernatural.

Many events will soon happen on earth, and I want to use a special breed of Christians. I want people with a lot of experience in heaven to work one on one with people on earth. The people on earth have to embrace the great cloud of witnesses as they are integral to this last great move I am going to do on earth. Many saints in heaven have not completed their destinies and have to co-labor with people on earth to fulfill their destiny and purpose.

What you are doing will be common for people to do in years to come. In 20 years, so many people will be doing it, and these series of books will seem groundbreaking for the time that they were produced. However, they won't be new information to those that read them 20 years from now.

Matthew:

This is easy to fathom. I love how you and the saints speak to me in clear language and in a way that I can understand.

Jesus:

You should never have to strain to understand me, Matthew. I only spoke in parables so that the hungry would seek God for the meanings. Few Christians really understand the parables even today. If they do understand, they don't seem to be taking my advice and living their lives according to the way that I suggested.

I will always speak clearly to you. I won't speak in hidden language or dark speech to you because I want to communicate with you, use you and have you affect other people.

Elijah:

2 Timothy 3:7 tells us that the people are always learning but never coming to the knowledge of the truth.

This is a sad way for the world to be. The world has so many teachers, trying to teach people, but for the most part, they are teaching what itching ears want to hear. The people of God have gathered under teachers that say what they want to hear.

The hard things, the meat of the Word, are largely neglected in this world. So many people are hungry for new revelation, but the revelation that they will find is that people need to live the way that Jesus taught and how he commanded his disciples to live.

It is sad that Jesus is revered as Savior but not as Master, Rabbi, Teacher or Lord. Everyone knows that to get a degree in any field, you have to study a subject and then show that you know the subject that you have been taught before you are given a passing grade. But sadly, the fact of the matter is that you can be called a Christian and revered as a Christian teacher and not even know what Jesus taught, let alone practice his teachings.

Let us have a look at a few words from the Master that Christians say that they follow. This is meat. I will quote the text and have you put each verse there and my commentary between each verse.

Luke 14:26-35

26 *"If anyone comes to Me and does not hate his father and mother, wife and children, brothers and sisters, yes, and his own life also, he cannot be My disciple."*

The whole message of Jesus can be summed up with loving God with all your heart, mind and soul and loving your neighbor. Jesus would not go through his whole ministry teaching love and then say to hate people.

Jesus is saying clearly here that you should not love your loved ones with the **same** love with which you love him. Jesus is saying that you should deny these relationships for him. When a choice comes up between them and him, they should be sacrificed.

This does not mean that you should live a life that is focused on ministry and then neglect your wife and family, but it means that Jesus and his ways should always be your first love. Jesus is saying deny your affections for all these people and even your own flesh to follow him. Few people are prepared to do this.

27 *"And whoever does not bear his cross and come after Me cannot be My disciple."*

People should see that you are carrying your cross as Jesus did. People should know that you are a Christian by the way you live your life. Your life should be laid down for the purposes of God. You should use your time, energy and resources to do what Jesus wants and not what you want. Of course, when you are properly aligned with God, you will only want what Jesus wants.

28 *For which of you, intending to build a tower, does not sit down first and count the cost, whether he has enough to*

finish it— 29 *lest, after he has laid the foundation, and is not able to finish, all who see it begin to mock him,* 30 *saying, 'This man began to build and was not able to finish'?"*

Very few Christians are told that the Christian life is a hard one and that it will cost them everything that is important to them. We have teachers who preach sermons to people with itching ears, so few people today are told that the proper Christian life is costly.

Just to produce this book, Matthew has to lay down his money, his time and his reputation in the world. Everything that Matthew has achieved in his life has cost him dearly. He does not enjoy it when we preach hard words to people. But now that we have your attention, this is a place where you can hear the truth.

The reason that non-believers are not interested in the Christin faith is that they see Christians who are saying they believe in Jesus, but they are not acting like the Jesus that they have heard about. These people of the world see Christians who have a half-completed building without the funds to finish the job. To them, the building is clearly half finished, but the Christians have no idea that they have an uncompleted building.

31 *"Or what king, going to make war against another king, does not sit down first and consider whether he is able with ten thousand to meet him who comes against him with*

twenty thousand? 32 *Or else, while the other is still a great way off, he sends a delegation and asks conditions of peace."*

Once again, the Christian life has a cost to it. Your Christian life will not work as it should if you are not prepared to pay the price.

33 *"So likewise, whoever of you does not forsake all that he has cannot be My disciple."*

Doesn't that sound like what Jesus said to the wealthy ruler? Jesus calls you to forsake everything to be his follower. You can try to live the Christian life and not forsake all, but that means that you are not a true disciple and that your life won't be a light or witness to other people. You won't make life taste good for others or preserve the quality of life on earth for them. Salt enhances flavor and preserves quality, and when you don't really become a disciple, you are a Christian in name only like salt that has lost its effectiveness.

34 *"Salt is good; but if the salt has lost its flavor, how shall it be seasoned?* 35 *It is neither fit for the land nor for the dunghill, but men throw it out. He who has ears to hear, let him hear!"*

Perhaps this is new to you. Perhaps you have heard these passages preached differently. Perhaps you have never considered yourself this flavorless salt. Many readers of this book might need to seek God now as this has convicted them.

How you forsake all, how you make Jesus your first love, how you follow after Jesus as a disciple is another subject for another time, but if in any way the Holy Spirit is tugging on your heart to confess to him and seek change, make sure that you do that now.

John the Baptist came with my spirit. He did not have my soul, but he came in the same spirit. If you read many of Matthew's writings, you will see that he, too, has my spirit within him.

Do you see that Jesus does not call you to a life of compromise? John came and preached repentance through baptism to the world before Jesus to prepare the hearts of men for the message and the life that Jesus was going to teach. I am calling you to change the way that you live.

Jesus is coming back for a pure, holy and set apart Bride. Jesus is coming back for a Bride that is unspotted by the world. Unspotted means that none of the ways of the world are in you. If you want to get your life right with Jesus, you are going to have a lot more fulfilling life.

Matthew, I know that this is hard for you. But we want to change the world. We want these books to bring a message of change. We want people to not only enjoy what you write, but we want a portion of your readers to make real changes in their lives. Sure, we want to change you also, and we have impacted you by what some of us have said to you, but this message has to be shared with people because many of them don't seem to be hearing it from their teachers.

Matthew:

It is hard for me to type and release, but that is part of being a servant to Jesus. I know some people will have a hard time swallowing this, but like medicine, it is good for people to have. I want to always be about the business of heaven. I really love these encounters, and this message that you have just shared, Elijah, is so important.

Bob:

Well, that is it for today. Not every message you give will be easy reading or simple to digest. We are here to change people and help them grow up in the faith and prepare them for what is coming to the earth. We are not here to play church as usual.

Matthew:

Bye, people.

(Elijah bowed to me and gave me a salute.)

Thanks, people.

Bob:

That was interesting.

Matthew:

Yes. I am coming to realize that what is said each day isn't on my agenda but follows the agenda of heaven. Thanks for today.

Message 15

Bob:

How are you today, Matthew?

Matthew:

Similar to most days, it is taking me some effort to get into the mood to ascend. I sense so much attack over this. I can't attribute these challenges to anything else. I guess people struggle the same way when it comes to prayer and reading the Bible. They are good things to do and very helpful, yet many people have negative emotions when they think about it.

Bob:

As with everything worthwhile, you have to push through. I saw that you were ready now, so I came for you. Shall we ascend?

Matthew:

(Wow. I am greeted by the Father. He hugs me and shows me to my seat.)

I am overcome. God is here!

Father:

You didn't think I would miss out on this, did you, my son?

Matthew:

I was guessing that you see everything and are aware of everything. I am so shocked that you are here. I am so blessed.

Father:

I have missed talking to you. You have completed "Conversations with God: Book 1" and "Conversations with God: Book 2," and you have started this book. I want you to continue with Book 3. I have come here to remind you to continue with them. I enjoy speaking to you and your readers.

How do you like this arena that you are in?

Matthew:

It is amazing. What is amazing is that any saint that I think of can come and speak to me here. That makes my mind spin. I am overwhelmed at what you are doing in my life. I know others that are reading would like to come here and speak to people like I do.

Father:

I built this for you. I want you to come up here often. I have a guest for you that wants to speak to you and to others. I will be sitting here and watching as you speak to him.

Jonah:

Hello, Matthew. Yes, I am the one that was swallowed by a big fish. People assume that the animal was a whale. I will let that mystery stay.

Do you know what I admire about you?

Matthew:

That I will do what God shows me to do each time that he shows me?

Jonah:

Yes, that is part of it, but there is more. The reason that you do what God tells you to do is because of your love for him and the people of the world. It is because of your love that you do what you do.

Like yesterday, in Message 14, you allowed Elijah to share about the cost of following Jesus. That was a tough message for people. It was not the cotton-candy message that some people are used to. It was the meat of the Word. You were having a hard time typing it and releasing it to your readers.

I am so impressed that you don't shrink back from what God calls you to do. It is because you care for that small percentage of people that are going to read a message like that and have a change of heart.

People know so well that I ran from doing God's will. People think that they would never do that. It's amazing how people read about a saint doing something wrong, and they think that they would never do the same thing.

Jesus shares the parable of the sheep and the goats. In that parable, he says what you do for the stranger or homeless, the hungry, the thirsty and the naked — the orphan and others — is what you do for him.

In big cities, people walk past the homeless every day without stopping and giving them some comfort. Do you know that many times, these homeless ones are angels and Jesus himself in multiple bodies? Do you know when the rewards are being handed out in heaven and people are wondering why they are not getting the rewards that they think they should receive that videos of them walking past Jesus will be played for them? Many people will be really surprised in that day.

Every time that this happens, whenever people walk past the hungry, naked and thirsty — the homeless that are dressed poorly — without a care for them, people are walking away from what God has called them to do. They are doing worse than what I did. At least I knew that I was running from God and his will. The people that ignore the poor in their midst think it is their right to ignore these poor souls and that God would never call them to minister to them.

Of course, God does not call you to feed every homeless person or to give a drink to all of them. But people need to wake up and see these people and have compassion on them. In loving these people, they are loving Jesus.

You have met Jesus four times in the flesh, Matthew. Each time you met him, he was dressed as a homeless man. It is your love for the homeless that has allowed you to meet Jesus that many times. If people wanted to have an encounter with Jesus or an angel, they would do well to start to take an interest in the poor in their midst.

Bob told you that churches have not invited you to preach at the moment because your message is too hard for them to take. Once again, today you are bringing a hard message. People don't like to feel guilty, yet how are the homeless ever going to see the light and love of Jesus if the people of God don't go to them? I have many things to say to you.

I enjoy people that know how to worship God in the things that they do with their lives and not just in song at church. I enjoy watching those who are vessels of love to all sorts of people as they go through their week. I enjoy people who have submitted themselves to God and who have humbled themselves. I enjoy watching people who are the same person with everyone that they meet. I enjoy watching people shine the light of Jesus in this broken world.

You would think that this whole world and all the people in it were going to heaven by the way that many Christians live their lives. So many people never share the hope of Jesus with anyone. God gives people many opportunities, and time and time again, they don't act on them. People look at me and see that I didn't give a message of warning to Nineveh, but Jesus told his followers to make disciples, and so few people actually do that. Many people who attend church have not shared the hope of Jesus with anyone in the last year.

You have a book that shares how a person can prophesy to strangers and bring them the hope of God called, "Prophetic Evangelism Made Simple." You go into a lot of detail on how they can make their heart right and be a good witness to people in that book. I wish that every Christian could get a hold of that book.

Like I said, you would think that the whole world was already going to heaven by the way that Christians live and interact with others.

Being a witness is as simple as listening to a person's cares and troubles and instead of leaving it at that, offering to pray for them. It is very rare that even a non-Christian will refuse prayer. You can pray a prayer of consolation and ask God to intervene in their situation, and you can watch God answer that prayer and see the whole attitude of the person change when your prayer is answered.

You can be a witness in so many ways in your life. You can show people love and have compassion on them. You can do something that is rare in the world; you can refuse to gossip and tell people that you are not going to have any part of it. Simply telling people that you are not going to participate in it might hurt them in the short term, but it will make an impact on them. When they are searching for love and a listening ear in the future, those people will come to you because they know that you will keep their troubles and concerns private.

There are few negatives in my story in the Bible, and I am sure that you have heard preachers preach on them and give life lessons from it.

Please listen to me.

The world out there wants to hear about Jesus and the way that he can transform their lives and give them peace and comfort. The world out there wants to know that they have a purpose and that they were created for a reason. The world out there wants to feel the love of God. Are you going to go to them and share the hope of Jesus with them?

Matthew:

Is it ever going to change, Jonah? Can you tell me about the future? Is the church ever going to go out to the highways and byways and bring in the people to meet God?

Jonah:

Yes, you will see some Christians who learn how to love God in an extraordinary way. These Christians will be set on fire, and they will be witnesses to the ends of the world. Christians are coming who will take the Gospel to the world. They will be special and be anointed for the task. You speak about that group of people in your book, "Optimistic Visions of Revelation."

But God is after more than these special, called-out ones to reach the world. God is after each saint in the world to make a difference. He is after everyone to go out and show his love to the world. He wants people to take up their cross, deny themselves and take the good message of the Gospel to the world. You addressed this beautifully in your book, "Influencing Your World for Christ."

Of course, God in his love and compassion isn't going to send his Son back to the world to collect his Bride yet. Of course, a group of people will witness to the world with power and all signs and wonders following. But he wants every Christian to be a witness. He wants every Christian to step out and touch someone. He wants so many things to happen and for everyone to be involved.

Matthew:

Are you honored to speak today?

Jonah:

Yes, I was so happy to speak today. I hope people don't get me wrong. I love the church. Jesus would love people to obey what he taught in the parables. Your book, "The Parables of Jesus Made Simple," is a good book to get an understanding of what Jesus was teaching. People need to understand that the Christian life is more than going to church and praying every day. The Christian life should be one of love, compassion and service. The Christian life should be one of giving and sacrifice. The church should come out of their four walls and demonstrate love to the world outside that is perishing.

The saints only say hard things because these are desperate times. The world is fast becoming a world where the standards of the Bible are said to be outdated and rigid. People today think that if it makes you happy, then it is good. All sorts of sin are accepted and promoted as an acceptable way to live. Christians need to be light and salt to the world through words, love and understanding. The people that have chosen things that are condemned in the Bible need to be loved, understood and directed to the love of Jesus.

These times that you live in will grow worse and worse. The darkness is going to spread, and the people of the church will be tempted to shrink back even more. Today, people won't witness to their work colleagues for fear of reprisals, yet within 20 years, life will be much harder. People will need to be full of love and compassion and have faith and boldness to speak out and share Jesus.

The time to share Jesus is now. The time to learn how to prophesy to strangers is now. The time to read about what Jesus' parables mean and how to apply them in your daily lives is now.

Can you imagine being an actor and being so good at your vocation that you are chosen for a role that wins you an Academy award? Can you imagine the whole world cheering you on? Can you imagine continuing to act and being chosen for wonderful roles, and five years later, winning another Academy award? By winning two Academy awards, you are part of an elite group of people. Not many actors win one award, let alone two.

Wouldn't you want to share the keys to your success and how to act in such a way that turns the hearts of people with other actors, even the industry professionals that vote for best actor? Wouldn't you do others a disservice by going to your grave and not sharing your knowledge with aspiring actors?

That is how us saints feel when we are speaking to you in these interviews. We are not here to share cotton-candy messages with you. We are not here to make people feel good though we hope you do. We are here to share how to live a life that makes you perform as the best Christiaan that you can possibly be. We are here to share how to live a committed life so that when God is handing out the eternal rewards in heaven that you will receive the maximum rewards.

Much of what we share, Matthew already knows and lives. The reason we have chosen him to be the mouthpiece is that he understands the information that is being shared, so he is a good one to share it with you.

Matthew has written a lot of books that help people. We are not quoting his books so that others will read this book or so that he will become rich. We are quoting his books because they are valuable resources that you can go to for more information.

We want to champion you. We have gone before you, and now, we want to direct you in this life that you are living. Paul had a strong message of meat. Elijah after him had a strong message, and today, I have had one. If you continue to read, you can be sure that many of us will bring messages that will have you become an Academy award winner yourself.

Father:

How was that?

Matthew:

Once again, I have no idea who will speak and what they will say. I simply sit here and type away. This time, we only had one saint, and none of the 12 said anything. Jonah was a great person to give such a message. Many of us don't think we would be a Jonah, but most of us seem to already be acting that way without being aware of it.

Father:

I love you. Start to make time for your next "Conversations with God" book. Now, give me a hug.

(The Father embraces me and gives me the most smothering, all-inclusive hug possible.)

(The saints have all started to eat what looks like fried chicken. A good mood is in the air like a party is about to happen. I have the impression that everyone is getting in a festive mood. I am told that they are all going to watch the first debate between Hillary Clinton and Donald Trump today. It is two hours in earth time until the debate begins, but the party has started in heaven.)

Bob:

You ready?

Matthew:

Yeah.

Bob:

That was good, wasn't it? It was wonderful to listen to. You had better get back to working on "Conversations with God." See ya later.

Matthew:

Bye, Bob.

(Bob took off right away to go back to the party in heaven.

I followed him, and Whitney Houston is singing the American national anthem in the arena. The whole arena is silent, and the song brings tears to my eyes. God loves America.)

Message 16

Bob:

How are you doing?

Matthew:

I have been feeling funny and out of sorts for a couple of days. I am under attack and have been delayed from doing this, so I thought I would go down to the shop, buy a Coca-Cola and get down to it.

Bob:

That is what perseverance is all about. We can't always be in the mood. You are called to minister on earth plenty of times when you are not feeling up to it. You have to go within and find something to give to the people. Today is a day like that for you. Shall we ascend?

Matthew:

Yes, let's go.

(Jesus meets me and embraces me in a hug. It is a wonderful feeling, and I stay in the hug for a while.)

Jesus:

I am so proud of you, my friend. You have courage to write this series of books. You are also obedient to pursue this each time you come. I love you so very much.

You are a joy to me. I love how you are so compliant to my will. The enemy tries to stop you in every way that he can, yet you just seem to press through and come anyway. I want you to know that I am very happy with you. You please me in so many ways.

Matthew:

Thank you, Jesus. That means a lot to me. I love to please you.

Jesus:

Today, I am going to have John speak to your heart. I know that you will be blessed.

Matthew:

Okay.

John the Baptist:

You just took a shower, and in the shower, you sensed that I was going to speak with you. I am glad to be here and to be able to speak to you.

You have a purpose here on earth. You are here to introduce the world to Jesus Christ. Not the Jesus they read about or the One they hear preached about in their churches. But you are here to show them the living Jesus, the One that wants them to love him and obey his teachings on earth.

You have a role to represent Jesus to the church. The Jesus they think they know, and the one they think they follow, is different from the real Jesus.

Of course, people love Jesus. They love the Jesus that they know. And yet, Jesus calls people to the narrow road if they are to follow him, and your job is to show people the narrow road.

Jesus said that wide is the road that leads to destruction. The sad thing is that this wide road is preached in many churches. The narrow road, the one that Jesus explained, is somewhat harder to follow, and a lot fewer people take it.

The fact that few people take this road does not mean that it cannot be found and followed by people that are on the wide road. Though the narrow road might be harder to pursue, the fullness of joy is found there. There is real joy in the right path.

Some might say, what is the right path? What is the narrow road that I am not following?

The path is following Jesus in all that he said and taught. The path is not just knowing about Jesus; it is about knowing Jesus personally and being directed by him day by day. It is not about being recognized in name as a Christian; it is learning how to be Jesus to your generation.

Matthew:

This is true. This is what I am about. I am always teaching people to look up the 50 commands of Jesus and for them to follow his commands. I have two books on intimacy with Jesus.

John the Baptist:

Yes, you are going to teach people about the 50 commands of Jesus. You are going to write a book about them one day. The people of God need to come away from routine and religious practices, and they need to get to know Jesus and communicate with him and emulate him with their lives on earth.

The path might be simple to define and to outline to people, but even with the path laid out, people still need to choose to follow it. This is where your teaching and the Holy Spirit's anointing come in to persuade the people to take the steps that it will take people to leave the wide road and come onto the narrow road.

The sad thing is that many people that are Christians think that they are already on the narrow road. Many of them think that since they became a Christian, they entered the narrow road. These people assume that what they are doing is right, so they are not even looking to change anything in their lives.

That is why we need you to show people that there is a better way to live. That is why we need you to show people that you can change and be in communion with Jesus every day and be led by him in all that you do and say. Rather than just sharing what people need to change and how they need to change, we are going to have you also share what you are up to and how your life is different so that people yearn for change.

Not everybody walks and talks to saints, angels and Jesus. Not everybody has a supernatural life. Many times, the people of God have no idea what their purpose is. For people to see that you know your purpose, that you walk with peace and joy and that you live a supernatural life might be something that will make a person want to know how you do it.

The people that are not walking in the narrow way have no idea that this is the case, and for a large part, this is not their fault, but the fault of their previous teachers. Preachers all around the world are sadly blind to the ways of Jesus and teach rules and religion rather than what Jesus taught. The people of God need to be led by those that know the way, and they have to learn to talk to Jesus and be directed by him.

Matthew:

This sounds like what I know I have to do. Thank you for reviewing it with me. I am happy that heaven agrees about what I am here for and what I am supposed to do.

John the Baptist:

You need to be clear about your purpose. It will take time and patience for you to teach this message, year after year. Your books will return to the same theme over and over again. You have already noticed that the Holy Spirit repeats these same themes. People might need to be told more than once.

I, the prophet who announced Jesus, even went into a period of doubt about him, and I sent my disciples to ask Jesus if he was really who he said he was. The record of that in the Scriptures should come as a warning to people that life can be hard, and pressures can even make you doubt your own words and your own purpose.

Times will come in your life, Matthew, when you will wonder if you are really making a difference. Times of attack will come when you are going to just get sick and tired of saying the same thing over and over again. You are going to wish that you had something new to share rather than simply directing people to Jesus and his ways, but you will have to persist. Of course, Jesus will have you share many revelations that will be new and fresh, but in the course of sharing them, you will also have to share the message that people need to obey him and follow him.

You see, Matthew, people are happy to run after revelation and new insights from heaven, and they will run after them all day but to be told to read the Gospels and to make sure they obey what Jesus taught is not too attractive to them.

People will read your books and say that you are a broken record in a review. They will be people that have read a number of your books and who have seen the common theme of obeying Jesus' commands and leaving the world behind to become set apart.

I want you to know that we are behind you in all of this. You can imagine how Jesus feels when people honor him in praise and worship, yet they refuse to obey what he taught. Can you imagine being the world's most famous teacher and the God of many denominations yet seeing many of your followers not doing what you taught?

I want you to share to share the link to the 50 Commands of Jesus in the online version of the article here:

http://ezinearticles.com/?The-Fifty-Commands-of-Jesus&id=468177

Okay, that is what I wanted to say. Goodbye for now.

Matthew:

Goodbye, John.

Jesus:

Are you okay with the fact that we are going to use you to point people back to me and my commands?

Matthew:

Someone has to do it, Lord, because few people understand that it must be done. People seem to have no idea that obeying you is the way to be a proper Christian. That is the way that we are going to change the world. That is the way that we are going to make a difference.

I am sure that you will allow me to write on many things to give me some variety, but I can see that I will have a common theme to speak about.

Thank you, Jesus.

Jesus:

That is enough for today. You did well. You were fighting all the way through to keep concentrating. I am glad that you persisted. Bye, now.

Matthew:

Bye, Jesus. Bye, John. Bye, saints.

Bob:

That was a shorter one today. You did very well. You can proofread it and post it now.

Matthew:

Thanks, Bob. I like that cowboy hat and straw sticking out of your mouth. It's cute.

Bob:

Ha ha. Just seeing that you are looking at me. See you later.

Closing Thoughts

Well, that was an exciting journey for me! I am three messages into the next book and really well on this path. I am enjoying myself during my visits to the galactic council, and it is my prayer that you will continue on the journey with me.

It is my understanding that God will allow the 12 saints in the council and the visiting saints from the arena to lead us and teach us the proper and correct way to live our Christian life in the 21st century.

Many of the things that the saints have been saying so far are known to me, and the saints seem to be using me as a mouthpiece since I have some understanding of what they are sharing. I can envisage that I am going to learn a lot also, and I have to say that I really enjoy going to heaven each time that I visit.

I look forward to speaking to some of the saints of the Bible and to the saints that have passed from more recent times. I can see that we will speak to Sadhu Sundar Singh and perhaps Smith Wigglesworth and John G. Lake in coming books. I hope also to speak to Charles Finney, Kathryn Kuhlman and others. I encourage you to join my

Facebook groups so that you can see when the next books in the series are free on Kindle.

It is my prayer that this book has blessed you, and I hope that you can return and reread it from time to time.

I'd love to hear from you

One way that you can bless me as a writer is by writing an honest and candid review of my book on Amazon. I always read the reviews of my books, and I would love to hear what you have to say about this one.

Since I read a lot of books, I always make sure to read the reviews of any books before I buy them. You can easily make a good decision about a book when you have read enough honest reviews from readers. One good way to make sure this book sells well and to give me positive feedback is to write a review for me. It doesn't cost you a thing but helps me and the future readers of this book enormously.

To sow into my book-writing ministry, read my blog or to request your own personal prophecy or life coaching from me, you can visit h*ttp://personal-prophecy-today.com* You can also request a guided trip to heaven. All of your gifts will go toward the books that I write and self-publish.

To write to me about this book, please feel free to contact me at my personal email address at *survivors.sanctuary@gmail.com*

You can also friend request me on Facebook at Matthew Robert Payne. Please send me a message if we have no friends in common as a lot of scammers friend request me.

You can also do me a huge favor by sharing this book on Facebook as an enjoyable book to read. This will help me and other readers.

Other Books by Matthew Robert Payne

The Parables of Jesus Made Simple

The Prophetic Supernatural Experience

Prophetic Evangelism Made Simple

Your Identity in Christ

His Redeeming Love- A Memoir

Writing and Self-Publishing Christian Nonfiction

Coping with your Pain and Suffering

Living for Eternity

Jesus Speaking Today

Great Cloud of Witnesses Speak

My Radical Encounters with Angels

Finding Intimacy with Jesus Made Simple

My Radical Encounters with Angels- Book Two

A Beginner's Guide to the Prophetic

Michael Jackson Speaks from Heaven

Conversations with God: Book 1

7 Keys to Intimacy with Jesus

Conversations with God: Book 2

Influencing Your World for Christ

Coming Soon

My Visits to the Galactic Council of Heaven: Book 2

My Visits to Heaven – Lessons Learned

Deep Calls unto Deep

You can find my published books on my Amazon author page here:

http://tinyurl.com/jq3h893

About the Author

Matthew was raised in a Baptist church and was led to the Lord at the tender age of 8. Matthew has known some pain and darkness in his life, which has led him to have a deep compassion and love for all people.

Today, he runs two Facebook groups, "Open Heavens and Intimacy with Jesus" and "Prophetic Training Group." Matthew has a commission from the Lord to train up prophets and to mentor people in the Christian faith. He does this by ministering to people through his groups and by writing relevant books on Christian living.

God has commissioned him to write at least 50 books in his life, and he spends his days earning the money to self-publish and fulfill that plan. You can support him in his ministry by donating to him at *http://personal-prophecy-today.com* or by taking advantage of the other services available on his website.

It is Matthew's prayer that this book has blessed you, and he hopes that it will lead you into a deeper and more relevant relationship with God.

Blurb

The writer of this book experienced hundreds of encounters with the great cloud of witnesses before he first met Bob Jones in a vision. Bob visited him three times over a couple of years, and then one day, he told Matthew to sit down and type and record their conversations. He was going to call the encounters "Conversations with Bob" and produce a book, knowing that the discussions would benefit others. Suddenly, Bob changed gears and started to take him to heaven.

Before Matthew knew it, he was speaking to 11 saints in heaven along with Jesus, and the name of the book was soon "My Visits to the Galactic Council of Heaven." The saints were happy to meet Matthew and only too aware that the conversations were being recorded to form a book, so they spoke to both Matthew and the intended readers, which will hopefully include you.

Heaven and the saints have change on their mind. Heaven wants to talk about what it is like to be a disciple and how to live a productive and successful Christian life on earth. This series of books, of which this is the first, will be a course in heavenly discipleship through the personalities and the wisdom of heaven's saints, who have been watching all of us on earth.

Come and see the personalities of heaven, come and listen to their instruction and their counsel, and if you are really eager and courageous, come and visit the council for yourself and ask your own questions. Let this book take you to heaven and be a stepping stone in your own personal encounters with the saints and Jesus in heaven.

www.ingramcontent.com/pod-product-compliance
Ingram Content Group UK Ltd.
Pitfield, Milton Keynes, MK11 3LW, UK
UKHW020142250726
13967UKWH00002B/807

9 781684 112524